Governors'
Mansions
of the Midwest

Governors' Mansions of the Midwest

Ann Liberman

Photographs by Alise O'Brien

University of Missouri Press
Columbia and London

Copyright © 2003 by
The Curators of the University of Missouri
University of Missouri Press, Columbia, Missouri 65201
Printed and bound in China
5 4 3 2 1   07 06 05 04 03

        Library of Congress Cataloging-in-Publication Data

Liberman, Ann, 1940–
    Governors' mansions of the Midwest / Ann Liberman ; photographs by Alise O'Brien.
        p. cm.
    Includes bibliographical references (p.) and index.
    ISBN 0-8262-1478-9 (alk. paper)
    1. Historic buildings—Middle West. 2. Historic buildings—Middle West—Pictorial works. 3. Mansions—
Middle West—History. 4. Mansions—Middle West—Pictorial works. 5. Governors—Dwellings—Middle West—
History. 6. Governors—Dwellings—Middle West—Pictorial works. 7. Governors—Middle West—Biography. 8.
Middle West—History, Local. 9. Middle West—Politics and government. 10. Middle West—Biography. I. Title.

F351.L53 2003
725´.17´0977—dc21

                                                                        2003050732

♾™ This paper meets the requirements of the
American National Standard for Permanence of Paper
for Printed Library Materials, Z39.48, 1984.

Design and Composition: Jennifer Cropp
Printer and binder: Everbest Printing Co. through Four Colour Imports, Ltd. Louisville, KY.
Typefaces: Minion, Granjon, and Medici Script

To Lee
My home sweet home

Contents

Acknowledgments

Many individuals have helped to make this project possible. From the beginning I have enjoyed the continuing guidance of the following professionals, each of whom liked the concept at once. I value them as friends: James Olson, President Emeritus of the University of Missouri; Professor Wayne Fields of Washington University; Dr. Robert Archibald, President of the Missouri Historical Society; Julius Hunter, Vice President at St. Louis University; and Dr. James Goodrich, President of the State Historical Society of Missouri. I also thank Dean Cynthia Weese of the Washington University School of Architecture; although she is a newcomer to the project, I have been listening to and learning from her for years.

I am also grateful to the University of Missouri Press and its great staff, including Beverly Jarrett, Jane Lago, Karen Renner, Dwight Browne, and Julianna Schroeder; they have helped me enormously, and their efforts have made this project possible.

Wonderful individuals in each of the states helped to make things run more smoothly. I called upon some of the researchers and curators countless times. I visited all of the mansions (except South Dakota) at least twice, and many of the mansion managers, curators, and others changed between my visits. I sincerely thank them all: in Illinois, Nita Crews and Thomas Martin; in Indiana, First Lady Judith A. O'Bannon, Nancy Cira, Jonathon Swain, Dana Denkiunas, and Suzanne Crowe; in Iowa, David Cordes, Bonnie McElroy, and Elaine Estes; in Kansas, Jennie Adams Rose and Karen Northup; in Michigan, Dan Crow; in Minnesota, Sherry Jacobsen, Tom Oehler, and Bill Suchy; in Missouri, Mary Pat Abele; in Nebraska, Karen Toussaint and Gail DeBuse Potter; in North Dakota, Steve Sharkey, Fern Swenson, and Claudia Berg; in Ohio, Kylie Towers, Julie Stone, Bobbie Wiard, Mary Alice Mairose, and Carl Pernotto; in South Dakota, Heather Bigeck, Gloria Guericke, and John Moisan; and in Wisconsin, Carrie Ballweg. I thank the South Dakota Department of Tourism for providing the interior photos of its executive residence; we respect the privacy of the governor and his family.

My deepest gratitude, however, is for Alise O'Brien, Lee's beautiful daughter, whose incredible photography graces the pages of this volume, and to her assistants, Matt Hughes and Teanne Chartrau. I thank my sons, Peter and Andrew Medler, Becca, and my husband, Lee Liberman, for their determination to pull me into the computer age. Their enthusiasm, patience, and endless humor have been my mainstay. I give thanks to the memory of my mother, who didn't get to read the book she encouraged me to write.

Governors' Mansions
of the Midwest

Introduction

When starting this book I thought it would be logical that our nation's governors' mansions would reflect a regional look. I expected to find that Midwest residences would be distinctive from those in other parts of the country. On the contrary, what I found is that popular architectural styles influenced governor's mansion construction as well as general home construction throughout most of the country. Cynthia Weese, dean of the School of Architecture at Washington University, recently told me: "The largest influence on the construction of houses in the Midwest was the East Coast. In other words, if you are building a mansion you look to other mansions. In the early years of this growing country there really was no regionalism. Regional architecture did not come to the Midwest until the twentieth century when it had its start in Chicago with Frank Lloyd Wright."

This country, which came together in a revolution against the monarchy of England, has been ambivalent about housing its governors in great style. On the one hand, we wanted to provide our governors with the kind of housing they needed in which to live, work, and entertain in a manner befitting both their status and the image we wanted to create for our state. But on the other hand, our roots discouraged implications of aristocracy.

Most of this bias was set aside, however, as the states sought to establish their identity and legitimacy. During the settlement years, territories and new states lacked an Anglo-European history. In developing an Americanized political and social hierarchy, they sought ways to show the rest of the nation that their population had become "settled" and "civilized." By providing a house for their governors, the states not only created new traditions, but also erected visible symbols of their progress.

Another discovery from my research is that many first ladies shared an urge to leave their mark on a house. They redecorated, they painted, and they made additions small and large. Their alterations emerged from a combination of "nesting instinct" and a wish to put their own "stamp" on the house.

When Jackie Kennedy undertook the restoration of the White House in 1961, she did so with the help and advice of Henry F. du Pont, creator of the Winterthur Museum in Delaware. At that time there was no White House curator, but Mrs. Kennedy formed the White House Historical Association and thereby brought national attention to the historical interiors. Her actions inspired first ladies all over the country to form mansion-preservation groups, and her influence continues. Mrs. Kennedy encouraged an interest in restoration and motivated first ladies to adopt standards for restorations that would add to the historical legacy of their state mansions.

The oldest house in the United States still in use as an official governor's residence is the Virginia mansion, built in 1813. The oldest in the Midwest that is continuously used for that purpose is the Illinois residence, built in 1855; it is the only midwestern governor's mansion that was built before the Civil War. Shortly after the Civil War, the Iowa and Missouri houses were built, the former as a private home and the latter as an official governor's residence. All of the midwestern states joined the Union in the nineteenth century, and all but Illinois, Iowa, and Missouri built their present-day governor's mansions in the twentieth century.

State and Mansion Reference

State	Joined Union	Current Governor's Mansion Completed
Illinois	1818	1855
Indiana	1816	1928
Iowa	1846	1869
Kansas	1861	1928
Michigan	1837	1959
Minnesota	1858	1912
Missouri	1821	1871
Nebraska	1867	1958
North Dakota	1889	1960
Ohio	1803	1925
South Dakota	1889	1936
Wisconsin	1846	1928

Five states built houses as dedicated governors' residences: Illinois, Missouri, Nebraska, North Dakota, and South Dakota. Generous benefactors donated houses for five states: Iowa, Kansas, Michigan, Minnesota, and Ohio. Two states—Indiana and Wisconsin—purchased their houses from private citizens.

In some cases there have been two or three mansions in the lifetime of the state, and in one case (Michigan), there are presently two mansions—one a summer mansion and the other a winter residence. In North Dakota, the original governor's mansion is now a museum maintained by the North Dakota Historical Society.

Some of the mansions are quite elaborate, while others are less so. Upon entering any these houses, however, I always feel a sense of awe, for each one was—and is—at the heart of its state's history. I am intrigued with the beauty and educational value of governors' mansions. These buildings tangibly connect the future to the past.

Although change is inevitable, it is nevertheless important to save enough of the old to preserve a sense of our heritage. Midwesterners can be proud of their successes in maintaining the historical integrity of their top executives' mansions while accommodating the change that comes with time. The stories of these homes continue, just as the lives of their residents go on and history unfolds.

Illinois
Governor's Mansion

National Register of Historic Places

Location: 410 East Jackson Street, Springfield

Construction Year: 1855

Cost: $35,500

Size: 6,250 square feet (currently 45,120 square feet)

Number of Rooms: 28 (currently 99 rooms)

Architect: John M. Van Osdel

Architectural Style: Modified Georgian

Furniture Style: English Regency

In the chaotic environment of most American frontier towns, fiery political frictions surrounded elections, and political patronage abounded. Frequent changes in territorial governors were not unusual. Some appointees resigned because they found the job too burdensome; others were fired or replaced with each change of the federal administration. Illinois, however, was different: In the nine years (1809–1818) that it existed as a territory, it was governed by only two territorial governors—with the first governor serving only twenty-one days and the second, Ninian Edwards, serving the remainder of the nine years. Edwards, a lawyer, was chief justice of the Court of Appeals in Kentucky at the time he was appointed by President James Madison to be the territorial governor of Illinois. Edwards and the first territorial governor, John Boyle, essentially traded jobs: Boyle become the chief justice in Kentucky when Edwards was sent to Illinois.

Illinois and Indiana were originally part of the Northwest Territory, but in 1800 they, along with Wisconsin and parts of Michigan and Minnesota, were split off from the Old Northwest to form the Indiana Territory. By 1809 the population of Illinois had grown so much that Congress decided it could stand on its own as a separate territory. The town of Kaskaskia, located on the southeastern edge of the territory, was named the first capital. In 1818 Illinois joined the Union, becoming the twenty-first state. As the population of the new state grew, Illinois officials sought a more central location for its capital than Kaskaskia, believing that settling a less populated site would spur the state's growth. They chose a new location in 1819, and in the following year they created a new town, named it Vandalia, and designed it as the state capital.

Springfield and Chicago had been established as towns in 1818, the same year that Illinois gained statehood. Both towns had grown rapidly, as had the population of the entire northern part of the state. Catering to the influence of northerners, the legislature decided to move the capital farther north to the center of the state. The Springfield city fathers offered a building site and fifty thousand dollars toward construction of the new capitol building, and in 1839 Springfield was selected as the state's capital, which it has been ever since.

State Representative Abraham Lincoln introduced legislation as early as 1840 to appropriate money for a residence for the governor. The bill didn't pass, and it was not until 1848 that the state purchased a two-story brick house, one block from Lincoln's home in Springfield, and designated it the official residence for the governor and his family. The house was small, plain, unpretentious, and of no architectural distinction.

Governor Joel A. Matteson, the tenth governor of Illinois and only the second governor to live in the Springfield house, had need of a larger house for his family of six children. Within one month of taking office in 1853, Governor Matteson convinced the legislature to appropriate eighteen thousand dollars for a new official residence. When the brand-new twenty-eight-room governor's mansion was built, completed and furnished, its cost totaled fifty-three thousand dollars—a significant cost overrun. This called for supplemental appropriations plus the use of a fund that had been created to cover general contingencies. In 1855, the completed mansion was the poshest place in Springfield, situated on a tree-covered slope, overlooking the dirt streets and wooden sidewalks of the rugged frontier town.

Illinois was settled by a heterogeneous population of Yankees and southerners. Northern Illinois had been settled mostly by Yankees, southern Illinois was settled mostly by southerners, and in the middle section Yankees and southerners overlapped. In terms of architecture, this heritage led to a mixture of styles throughout the state.

For example, the Illinois governor's mansion is an archetypical antebellum house reflecting that Springfield was settled by southerners. The 1855 mansion, a two-story red-brick Victorian-era house, is the oldest governor's mansion in the Midwest. The brick was manufactured in Springfield and was said to compare favorably with the best Baltimore and Philadelphia brick. Built in the modified Georgian style with Greek Revival interiors, the house is redolent of southern charm. Its style includes a combination of architectural elements. The bracketed eaves and sloping hip roof are Italian influences. Additionally, the original roof was capped with a fifteen-foot cupola. But the clustered columns and paired windows are Classical features that were also popular in the era.

The house sits on a lot of almost three acres, known in early days as "Cooks Grove." Originally it was a heavily wooded site where rural settlers shot game as a major source of food. But as Springfield flourished and its population spread, "Cooks Grove" became surrounded by downtown Springfield.

The governor's mansion remains one of the most captivating sights in Springfield. And like other governor's residences it has suffered from the problems of aging, frequent changes of occupants, and intermittently an occasional lack of attention, or excessive attention of the wrong kind, resulting in inappropriate additions or alterations. The signature architectural feature of the house is its grand spiral staircase, an elliptical wonder said to be matched by only one other in the United States. As an example of attention of the wrong kind, this unique staircase was removed and replaced at one time, but fortunately it was later reinstalled in accordance with the original building design. For another example, the house's red-brick exterior was painted white in its early years, but in 1971 an extensive restoration returned it to its original color.

The first professional architect to reside in Chicago, John Mills Van Osdel, designed the governor's residence. Van Osdel, son of a New York architect, established his Chicago practice and his reputation in 1837 by planning and creating buildings in the city of Chicago. One of his early commissions was designing a house for Chicago's first mayor. Van Osdel played a prominent role in creating early Chicago landmarks such as the Greek Revival Rush Medical College, the original courthouse, the Palmer House, and the Tremont Hotels, as well as important private homes.

Governor William H. Bissell, partially paralyzed and in poor health when elected in 1857, was the second governor to live in the new mansion. Bissell was inaugurated in the mansion, and because of his physical infirmity he was never thereafter able to leave the house. He conducted all of the state's business from the house and received all visitors there, including his close friend Abraham Lincoln. In 1860 Bissell died and his body lay in state for three days in the west parlor of the mansion's center vestibule. The funeral ceremony also took place in the mansion.

John Tanner served as governor from 1897 to 1901. His inauguration was considered the largest and most important social event in Springfield history. Cora Tanner, a Springfield socialite, and Governor-elect Tanner married just days before he took office as the last governor of the nineteenth century. By that time, over forty years had elapsed since the house had been built, and it needed significant renovation. The weak infrastructure was failing, and the plumbing required replacement. Even the beautiful spiral staircase, the hallmark of the mansion, was on the verge of collapse.

In 1897 Cora Tanner began a massive renovation, including the addition of several new rooms. The renovation was not always in keeping with the Greek Revival interior, and it was unfitting primarily because she removed the famous staircase and replaced it with something entirely different: The new staircase was square, not spiral, with landings and an adjoining alcove large enough to hold an orchestra. It was modeled after one in Fontainbleau Palace near Paris. Although the staircase was not intentionally made to resemble a Frank Lloyd Wright design, the combination of its squared-off horizontal aspect with the open space of the second-floor landing were elements that would typify Wright's architecture.

Praised in the newspapers for her personal style and handsome looks, Cora Tanner received public approval for almost everything she did. "The governor advised her to enjoy it all while it is yours to enjoy. For, he said, the public soon forgets who did what."[1]

There was little, if any, controversy surrounding the extreme changes she made in the governor's mansion. Even when she painted the woodwork of the mansion red, no one appeared to be offended or consider her outrageous; rather, the public seemed to think her changes to the mansion were smart and stylish improvements.

In general, alterations to the mansion generally reflected the differences in taste and styles of the first families who lived there. Many of these families were able to secure legislative appropriations for updating the mansion decor. As in some other states, there is evidence in Illinois of the aspirations of some of the first ladies to leave their mark on the mansion's decor or to change the aesthetics to satisfy their own standards. Governor Richard Yates Jr. (1901–1905) received a ten-thousand-dollar appropriation from the legislature for "furnishing and repairing," despite the fact that the huge renovation by the Tanners had just been completed when Yates took office. One piece of Tanner decor erased by Mrs. Yates was the covering of the woodwork's red paint by black paint and gold flecks.

1. John T. Trutter and Edith E. Trutter, *The Governor Takes a Bride: The Celebrated Marriage of Cora English and John R. Tanner, Governor of Illinois, 1897–1901,* 59.

The years passed and, by the time that Governor Dwight H. Green took office in 1941, the governor's mansion was eighty-six years old. It was apparent that difficult judgments regarding the functionality of the house had to be made. One of the floors was infested with termites, plaster was falling off in many rooms, some of the ceilings were deteriorating, and the interior walls were structurally deficient and in dire need of reinforcement.

The governor made the decision that the house's history, importance, and outstanding architecture should not be disregarded, and that the venerable old mansion should be put back together instead of being abandoned in favor of something new. The legislature agreed, the house was preserved, and every succeeding Illinois governor since 1941 has observed the preservation precedent set by Governor Green.

Adlai E. Stevenson became governor in 1949 and served a single four-year term as the twenty-first governor to occupy the mansion. There was no first lady in residence at the mansion, and during his term there was no push to redecorate, for he was busy launching his presidential race.

At the time Otto Kerner Jr. (1961–1968) became governor, the house was considered a firetrap and unsafe. With a sixty-five-thousand-dollar appropriation from the legislature, Kerner fireproofed the building, made roof repairs, and installed a fire escape and smoke screen. The smoke screen enclosed the stairway opening to prevent smoke from entering the mansion's top floors in case of fire. But the mansion needed more work than this: the place was over a hundred years old. Some in the state again strongly advocated that the mansion be sold and a new one be built on a site away from the downtown Springfield business district. The Executive Mansion Commission was then established to study and make recommendations to the legislature. The 1967 report of the commission led to a $1.5 million legislative appropriation for the preservation and expansion of the old building. When mansion restoration was researched by the architectural and engineering firm Graham, O'Shea, and Wisnosky, the firm reported that despite old age, the building was "not in extremely poor condition."[2] Governor Kerner, however, postponed the work because he felt the state lacked adequate funds.

Governor Richard B. Ogilvy (1969–1973) succeeded Governor Kerner and for a time continued to delay the renovation proposal out of concern for the enormity of the required financial commitment. The longer the project was delayed, however, the more the cost increased, and eventually $2.9 million was needed to do the project properly. In late 1970, construction began. The first phase involved the renovation and preservation of the original structure, and the second phase involved the construction of the new addition to the building.

During the Ogilvy administration, outstanding decorative changes were also made to the mansion. In the second-floor parlor called the Kankakee Room, the Ogilvys covered the walls with panoramic block-print French paper similar to that which Jackie Kennedy installed in the

2. Marie Magenheimer, "House-Hunting Again," *Springfield Journal-Register,* 1970; *Journal-Register,* December 31, 1972.

White House during the early 1960s. The richly colored and intricately patterned paper is beautiful, grand, and sophisticated. It tells a visual story about America's colonial days through the eyes of a Frenchman. Although greatly atmospheric, it is factually somewhat inaccurate.

Beginning with Governor Ogilvy, the restoration of the mansion progressed over twenty years and involved three administrations. It was the longest-running renovation in the Midwest, and the result is truly an outstanding mansion by any measure. According to the October 1993 issue of *Money* magazine, "Jim Edgar of Illinois lives in the largest manse (of any of our state governors), a 99-room, 45,120 square-foot behemoth that is nearly as big as the White House."[3]

But the *Money* article also pointed out that only 2,250 square feet, 5 percent of the building, is used exclusively by the governor and his family for their living space. The governor's private quarters contain a family dining room, four bedrooms, a sitting room, and a lounge. The public areas occupy most of the forty-two thousand square feet. As a state facility and the center of official social life, these public areas of the mansion are heavily used. The residence is a major tourist attraction visited by more than fifty thousand people annually.

In addition to a host of structural problems and technical reasons for rebuilding and restoring the house, other considerations played a part in the magnitude of the project. The museum-like finished product was partially guided by the museum quality of much of the mansion's inventory. The unique history of the house and the integrity of the interior and exterior architecture were also factors. The expansion project has preserved and enlarged the house's legacy as a repository for priceless objects with the Abraham Lincoln provenance and lineage.

George Healy, an American painter, made a series of portraits of early presidents that hang in the White House. The Lincoln family commissioned a copy of the artist's portrait of President Lincoln and it now hangs in the governor's mansion. A portrait of Mary Todd Lincoln by artist Francis Carpenter greets visitors in the first-floor parlor. Secretly commissioned by Mrs. Lincoln as a surprise for her husband, the artist ignored her request to destroy the unfinished portrait when the president was assassinated. There is also an oil portrait of Edward Baker, a close friend of the Lincolns, for whom they named their second child. It originally hung in the White House, and after Lincoln's death it was given to a Lincoln relative who later donated it to the mansion.

The only sculptor for whom Lincoln posed, Thomas D. Jones, modeled a bust of him smiling in 1860, just before his inauguration. It sits in the mansion library that is part of the new addition. The library's custom walnut-burl paneling, reported to cost fifty thousand dollars, was designed to complement the original Greek Revival style of the interior architecture of the house.

Some of the antiques that were original to the house or its earlier residents include paintings and china belonging to Mrs. Lincoln as well as an important antique table made in 1864 for President Lincoln by a man from Wisconsin named Peter Glass. This tabletop contains twenty

3. Walter L. Updegrave, "How Our Governors Live It Up," *Money*, 122.

thousand slivers of wood that fit together to form a beautiful mosaic. It stood in the White House until Abraham Lincoln's assassination and is now in a parlor of the governor's mansion.

Two of the residence's guest rooms have historical bedroom furnishings. The mahogany Lincoln bedroom suite was a gift to President Lincoln after his inauguration, but due to the massive size of the headboard and the dresser it could not fit into Lincoln's Springfield house. The other set is a carved oak Bartels bedroom and sitting-room suite. William J. Bartels, an Illinois farmer, hand carved the suite, which was originally exhibited at the Columbian Exposition in Chicago in 1893. It was purchased for the mansion at a Sotheby's auction in 1980. Each of these furnishings is a permanent part of the mansion's collection of antiques.

The governor's mansion is furnished with English Regency antiques to complement both the Greek Revival interior architecture and the Georgian exterior architecture, providing a transition between the two styles. There were a few Regency antiques and several reproduction pieces already in the house when renovation began. The majority of the antiques were collected in the early 1970s, most of them being European imports purchased at the shipping dock in New Orleans. The Springfield buyers actually went onto the ships in the port to make purchases for the mansion. Most of the very expensive and important accessories in the house were paid for through donations raised by Illinois citizens or have been donated by individual owners. One most generous donor, Robert Todd Lincoln Beckwith, who died in 1985, was Abraham Lincoln's great-grandson.

Although the house is now an up-to-date and efficient governor's residence by modern standards, it still retains the connection to its past through its history and its prominent historic contents. In 1976 the Illinois governor's mansion became an official historic site when it was placed on the National Register of Historic Places.

In response to the high cost of the mansion project, in 1972 Governor Ogilvy helped to establish the private, not-for-profit Illinois Executive Mansion Association to raise funds for furnishings and interior decor. The group was successful in raising over a half-million dollars, but of equal importance, the association has provided for careful regulation of all changes to the mansion so that no future first family will be able to alter its appearance without the association's approval.

The state of Illinois created a governor's residence that is a showplace as well as a museum. While the building and its furnishings show a side of Illinois history that is human and personal, it also offers insights into state government and politics. A visitor to the Illinois house can be overwhelmed by the amount of information presented about Illinois and its history as well as the architecture and furnishings of vintage houses.

The continuing preservation and maintenance of this house consolidates the new and old. Ever since the 1970s, the historic old building has been extremely well maintained. Of all the U.S. governors' mansions that have been continually used as the official residence of their governors, the Illinois mansion is the third oldest. Only Mississippi and Virginia have older buildings still in use.

Visitors' entrance under north portico of mansion.

Second-floor parlor, the Kankakee Room, with beautiful French wood-block documentary wallpaper, looking into guest room with Bartel furniture.

Elliptical stairway.

Parlor featuring English Regency furniture. This
is one of four parlors used for official entertaining.

Lincoln bedroom furniture created for the president in
1860 and given by the family to the governor's mansion.

One of the many formal gardens.

Indiana
Governor's Mansion

Location: 4750 North Meridian Street, Indianapolis

Construction Year: 1928

Cost: $242,000*

Size: 6,600 square feet

Number of Rooms: 16

Architect: Rubush and Hunter Architectural Firm

Architectural Style: English Tudor

Furniture Style: European antiques and reproductions

* Price paid by state in 1974. Original price is unavailable but is estimated at $40,000–50,000.

In 1800, when Congress divided the old Northwest Territory, the western portion was reorganized as the Indiana Territory. It included the present states of Indiana, Illinois, and Wisconsin, and parts of Michigan and Minnesota. The territorial capital was established at Vincennes and later relocated to Corydon. Twenty-seven-year-old William Henry Harrison, who had distinguished himself in the military during the early wars against the Indians, was appointed the first governor of the territory. He served as territorial governor for twelve years, quitting the post to fight in the War of 1812.

In 1811, while he was still governor, Harrison made a treaty with Indian officials to transfer almost three million acres of their land to the territory. The trade gave the Indians little in return, and it was denounced by the Shawnee chief Tecumseh. While Tecumseh was traveling to the South, Governor Harrison seized upon his absence by taking charge of the militia and driving the Indians from the territory in the famous Battle of Tippecanoe.

In 1816, Indiana officially entered the Union. Its huge territory had been subdivided in 1805 and again in 1809. The latter division, which separated Illinois from Indiana, left Indiana with almost the same boundaries it has today.

Once Indiana gained statehood, the location of its capital city, Corydon, proved inconvenient. Situated extremely far south, almost on the Kentucky border, it seemed poorly located for serving the growth of the state. In those early days, settlers relocated frequently, establishing new towns and abandoning other settlements. Anything from an outpost to an empty prairie could evolve to become a territorial capital or eventually a state capital. Many early capital sites were abandoned in favor of locations that could better enhance a state's future. Politicians in Indiana began looking at new sites in 1820; the following year, they selected a densely wooded tract of land next to the White River, almost at the center of the state. Thus before it ever became a town, the site was named Indianapolis, capital city of Indiana.

Alexander Ralston, a surveyor who had worked with Pierre L'Enfant to design Washington, D.C., was hired to lay out the city of Indianapolis. Drawing upon his previous experience, he modeled Indianapolis symmetrically, designing it with wide boulevards similar to those in Washington. In the center of a square mile of land he encircled a plot of four acres with a roundabout street eighty feet wide. The streets running north and south and east and west intersected with diagonal streets, making a grid. One of the major intersecting streets, Meridian, is today the beautiful avenue and landmark street in Indianapolis where the governor lives. Ralston designated the very middle of the circle, a slightly elevated knoll then shaded with sugar maples, as the site for the governor's residence.

Ralston envisioned the house as it would look among the maple trees, which would provide privacy and protection in a parklike setting. By 1827, six years after deciding on the city's location, when the Indiana legislature appropriated four thousand dollars to build a house for the governor, the maple trees had been sacrificed for firewood during the process of building and laying out the town. No longer quite a place of beauty, the knoll provided an overly exposed and stark setting for the governor's house. The completion of the big, square, yellow-brick house crystalized some earlier misgivings about its construction. Edward Eggleston, author of *The Hoosier Schoolmaster,* described it as "remarkable only for its homely bigness and dirty color." It remained controversial as long as it stood.

Although Governor and Mrs. James Brown Ray were to have been the first family to live in the new house, they never moved in. "Live in that house? No indeed! We would be under the eyes of everybody. Every woman in town would take account of our washing when we hang it out on Monday morning,"[1] said Mrs. Ray.

Poorly planned and impractical for family life, the house in Governor's Circle had neither a kitchen nor a pantry. No governor's family ever occupied it, and for the next thirty years it was used for state offices, and social events, including occasional inaugural balls. Crudely maintained, it eventually became derelict, and in 1857 it was auctioned for $667. Once the house was torn down, the site was used as a grazing pasture. Around 1870, it was cleared and fenced and became known as Circle Park, until its eventual transformation in 1901 into Monument Circle, which it is called today.

David Wallace was governor from 1837 until 1840. The Indiana legislature purchased a house, on the corner of Market and Illinois Streets, from Dr. John Sanders, father of Zerelda Wallace, the governor's wife. The legislature paid nine thousand dollars for the house, which was considered "the handsomest and most capacious dwelling house in the town."[2] In addition to Governor Wallace, the building housed several of his successors.

As Indianapolis grew and prospered, additional sidewalk construction and street grading became necessary. The new grading elevated the streets surrounding the governor's residence so that in rainy weather the mansion received the runoff, becoming encircled by water. Several occupants of the house suffered poor health. Governor James Whitcomb's wife died while living there, and the governor blamed the damp unhealthy environment in the house. The interior walls were often damp due to the standing water, and Governor Oliver P. Morton considered the house uninhabitable—in 1864 he moved to a hotel.

The old mansion and its grounds were sold in 1865, and for more than fifty years there was no official Indiana governor's residence. The length of time between residences was unprecedented and inconvenient. Many governors lived in hotels and boarding houses; others rented or purchased homes. Some governors changed addresses numerous times during their terms, moving from place to place as something better became available. Although the state considered various prospects for official residences, financial matters kept the state from approving the purchase of any.

By 1850 many affluent citizens had moved just north of Governor's Circle and built homes on lower Meridian. A portion of Meridian Street was the first to be paved with cedar blocks, and by 1870, cedar block was the paving material of choice, for it was quieter and smoother

1. Richard S. Simons, "White Elephant on the Circle," *Indianapolis Star Magazine,* December 21, 1952.
2. W. R. Holloway, *Indianapolis: A Historical and Statistical Sketch . . . ,* 64.

than gravel or stone. The handsome 1890s Meridian Street houses had large lawns and ornate iron fences. There were brick and gravel sidewalks and a mix of residences, churches, and public commercial buildings, all characteristic of the nineteenth-century neighborhood.

By 1880, Indianapolis was one of the most prosperous of midwestern cities. The coming of the railroad in 1855 heralded an age preoccupied with transportation. People demanded better streets and roads; chronicles from the era record great commercial strides: "Until the end of World War I, most of the automobiles . . . on all the roads of the United States were made in Indiana."[3] Used by pioneers moving West and in Gettysburg during the Civil War, Studebaker wagons became even better known when in 1902 Indiana's Studebaker company became famous for making automobiles.

In 1919 the Indianapolis Park Board purchased a Tudor Revival house, built in 1908, and leased it to the state to use as a governor's residence; governors lived there until 1945. Located at the juncture of Twenty-Seventh Street and the Fall River Parkway, it became a victim of rapid growth and urbanization. When, by 1943, the noise and dirt from the Parkway traffic disturbed the privacy of the house and its occupants, the legislature decided to seek a new residence for the governor.

From 1945 until 1973 an elegant buff-colored house at 4343 North Meridian Street served as the governor's mansion. The house was built in 1920 for the president of the Stutz Motor Car Company, William N. Thompson; by the time the state purchased it, it belonged to the J. H. Trimble estate. The state paid seventy-two thousand dollars for the house and many of the Trimble family furnishings. The most outstanding of these is a Steinway piano with ornately painted murals that coordinate with the colors of the room of its original environment. Today the piano is still a thing of beauty, and its polish, color, and design bring history into the living room of the present governors's residence.

The two-and-a-half story, twelve-room Renaissance Revival Trimble House was long and imposing, with one-story extensions on each end. Wrought iron trimmed its slate roof and second-story balconies.

After more than twenty-five years of official occupancy, the house's interior space proved inadequate and needed a costly overhaul, Governor Edgar D. Whitcomb and the legislature decided to sell the house. It brought fifty-two thousand dollars at auction in 1973.

In 1973 the Governor's Mansion Commission voted to buy a 6.5 acre estate several blocks north of the old residence, but also on Meridian Street. The state of Indiana purchased the estate from C. Severin Buschman in 1974 for approximately $242,000.

In the twentieth century, many homes on lower Meridian were replaced by commercial buildings, and the northern end of Meridian established itself as the fashionable residential avenue of grand homes replacing the farms and open country that had earlier extended beyond town. Wealthy families were building brick and limestone mansions on North Meridian.

3. William E. Wilson, *Indiana: A History,* 194.

Today the architecture of North Meridian represents a mix of revival styles that maintain the character of a substantial neighborhood developed for the upper and upper middle classes. The street has a uniform appearance because the houses have long and deep front lawns; restrictions pertaining to lot size and setbacks, and building specifications guarantee the visible coherence of North Meridian.

The official home of the Indiana governors is a 6,600-square-foot, sixteen-room English Tudor house. (The room count does not include storage rooms, dressing rooms, bathrooms, or closets.) Located at 4750 North Meridian Street and built in 1928, the governor's mansion reflects the popular Tudor Revival style that dominates the neighborhood. Almost two-thirds of the houses built in the vicinity of the governor's residence are of the Tudor Revival style, most of them being American versions of grand English manor houses. Yet the governor's house is unique in its understated appearance. It does have some of the manor-house features, including multigabled roofs and leaded windows, but there is no baronial sense of splendor. It is so subtle, so sweetly landscaped that it is reminiscent of an English cottage. But this house has great beauty in its refinement and subtlety.

The house is situated in a romantic setting where its acreage and landscape grant it privacy and a feeling of containment. Because the Tudor house has a sizeable acreage, one might expect it to feel like a grand estate mansion instead of this jewel of a house built into the landscape. The lovely design is well-balanced and orderly. The entire structure is reinforced concrete including the attic floor. Its sturdiness makes it exceptional even for the well-built 1920s Meridian Street houses.

The surrounding neighborhood was recognized as the North Meridian Street Historic District in 1971. In 1986, the North Meridian Street Historic District was listed in the National Register of Historic Places. There is also a Meridian Street Foundation, which plans activities to increase interest in preservation. Another group, the Meridian Street Historic Preservation Commission, has design review authority for the district.

A collection of period antiques and beautiful floors and oriental rugs define the interior of the Indiana governor's residence. From a French rococo mirror and a William and Mary chest to a well-preserved 1770s Chippendale breakfront with original glass, the house reveals a legacy from several administrations. Attractive reproductions are combined with the antique furnishings. Period pieces in the dark-wood-paneled library and the foyer reinforce the English Tudor style of the house. There is an outstanding Sheraton dining-room table and sideboard, three Sheraton benches, and an eighteenth-century grandfather clock. A stained-glass window created for the foyer is hypnotically beautiful; the artist combined fragments of opalescent glass with round disks of old glass from original skylights in the capitol building. City Glass Specialty, Inc., of Fort Wayne donated the leaded-glass window, which had taken nearly a year and a half to create.

The grounds overflow with blooming trees in spring, and a formal garden honors Indiana as the birthplace of famous writers. Some thirty-six authors, including James Whitcomb Riley,

Theodore Dreiser, Booth Tarkington, Lew Wallace, and Kurt Vonnegut, are memorialized, and their famous quotations are combined with plant identifications to designate thirty-six species.

During their occupancy of the governor's house, from 1981 to 1989, Governor and Mrs. Robert Orr initiated numerous projects to improve the house's appearance. The first lady, Josie Orr, a talented fund-raiser, found willing contributors to pay for the antiques, furnishings, and updating of the residence. She crisscrossed the state speaking to community groups and raising money for the residence.

In 1981 Josie Orr commissioned a gazebo to be installed on the lawn of the residence. It is a fourteen-foot-tall iron structure, twelve feet in diameter, with a domed roof. Looking like a bird cage, this circular piece of whimsical sculpture was built by the Gilpin Ornamental Iron Company and paid for by private sources. In the *Indianapolis News,* Josie Orr responded to those who criticized the commission: "People ask me why would I do something so crazy . . . I think it's fun. . . ." The article went on to explain, "Josie Orr doesn't mind if people laugh when they see the wrought-iron gazebo. That's why she put it there—to make people happy."[4]

Today the gazebo has become such a fixture that many people think it has always been there. Just as Josie Orr intended, it is whimsical, but it has also become an appreciated local artwork.

Governor and Mrs. Frank O'Bannon moved into the residence in 1996 and have actively promoted the use of the house for community forums. They host very large gatherings and are on the brink of a 2003 renovation that will enhance the accessibility of the mansion for people with disabilities. This change will add an entrance to the house on the south side of the building, and the present brick patio will become an interesting courtyard space. The new entrance will incorporate a new meeting and events room that can accommodate forty people for a sit-down dinner. This alteration will not only better serve the community as well as the residents of the house, but it will also provide a more gracious and easier entry.

How the governor's residence is utilized by the O'Bannon administration is best described by First Lady Judy O'Bannon, who says, "Everything we do here is on community-building. It is in doing things together that we become a community. It is important to use the residence for community outreach with all ages, and by encouraging community accomplishments, we motivate people to enter into partnership in any community in which they find themselves."[5]

The outdoors provides special opportunities for community events. An outstanding example is the Community Garden that hosts a summer day camp for at-risk students and the Indiana Juvenile Correctional facility. With the help of adult mentors who are gardeners, these youth learn by doing. They plan, design, create, and plant their garden, record their garden notes, and track their progress. To showcase their accomplishments and share their spirit, at an annual fall festival, they open their garden—as well as their hearts—and host several hundred guests.

4. "Orr's Sculpture Is for the Birds?" *Indianapolis News,* November 19, 1981.
5. First Lady Judith O'Bannon, interview by author, Indianapolis, October 24, 2002.

The historical heart of Indianapolis is Monument Circle. Regardless of whether it was called Governor's Circle or Circle Park, it has always been at the center of the city. Today it is the site of the Soldiers and Sailors Monument, a 285-foot-high limestone edifice crowned with a 38 foot bronze statue of Victory. This is a far cry from the original idea of using the location for the governor's mansion, but the area remains the grand hub of the city. The stunning monument, a 1901 Beaux Arts obelisk, reflects the ambitions of the citizens and reminds one of how far the city has come. "Indianapolis is like a museum or a fair exhibiting samples of a culture."[6]

Today, Indianapolis is bright; its streets are clean and the downtown buildings, whether new or old, are excellently maintained. The Capitol Commons Park, near the seat of state government, features fountains, walkways, and pergolas as part of the landscape; Monument Circle evokes the connection between the first governor's residence in Indianapolis and the present one; and the current governor's residence exudes a sense of community pride that seems to extend to the entire Indianapolis area.

From the first governor's residence at the circle to the present one on North Meridian Street, one observes the parade of passing history that parallels that of the state. In reinventing the plans for Governor's Circle and eventually finding a permanent home for the governor, Indiana residents have added to their history, kept up with the times, and preserved their past in a graceful and respectful way.

6. John Bartlow Martin, *Indiana: An Interpretation*, 8.

Living room with bay window and
with the elaborately painted piano
from the old governor's mansion.

The predominately blue and gold stained-glass windows
in the foyer. Some of the glass is from the capitol building.

Front hall featuring seventeenth-century, inlaid William
and Mary walnut chest and stairway.

This wooden squirrel statue was hand-carved from a backyard tree that had to be cut down.

View of the north entrance.

Iowa
Governor's Mansion

National Register of Historic Places

Location: 2500 Grand Avenue, Des Moines

Construction Year: 1869

Cost: $250,000 (including furnishings)

Size: 16,000 square feet

Number of Rooms: 20

Architect: William W. Boyington

Architectural Style: Second Empire

Furniture Style: Victorian era antiques

The Louisiana Purchase in 1803 included the land we now call the state of Iowa. The United States officially opened Iowa for settlement in 1833 and five years later gave it territorial status. Burlington served as the temporary territorial capital until a new town, Iowa City, was created as the official territorial capital. Later, after Iowa's statehood in 1846, the legislature decided the capital should be more centrally located, and it chose Des Moines.

Iowa became the twenty-ninth state to join the Union at a time when the United States was in the midst of turmoil: War with Mexico broke out. America was expanding rapidly, and its economy was changing from agricultural to industrial. Slavery was casting a long shadow of discord, adding to the chaos caused by war and industrialization. Yet Iowa joined the nation as a center of pastoral peace, an image it has more or less sustained throughout its history.

Then, as now, Iowa was characterized by this peacefulness. In the 1840s the Amish settled in Iowa in pursuit of religious freedom. Also in the forties, as Karl Marx was beginning to spread communism in Germany, a utopian communal-based German society moved to this country and eventually settled in Iowa, establishing the Amana Colonies. Most settlers from the east came to Iowa for the purpose of homesteading to establish farms. This calm, pastoral environment served to create the image of Iowa that remains solidly embedded in the American mind to this day. The famous covered bridges of Madison County were built by Iowa farmers between 1855 and 1885. The bridges also evoke the rural settings typically associated with Iowa.

Iowa did not provide its governors with a place to live for the first hundred years of statehood, except for the purchase of a modest house next to the capitol building in 1917 for the then-governor William L. Harding (who should not be confused with President Warren G. Harding, who was from Ohio). When none of the governors who succeeded Harding chose to live there, the house was used as a state office building.

Thirty years later, in 1947, the state purchased a rose-colored brick Dutch Colonial house to be used as an official governor's residence. The purchase price was $27,200, and the first governor to occupy it was Governor William S. Beardsley. Seven governors lived in the house before it was sold in 1977 to the Iowa Girls High School Athletic Union for $140,000.

The three-story, twelve-room house had been built in 1903 for the family of Dutch immigrant Gerald S. Nollen. Despite the architectural charms and beautiful interior woods of the house, by the 1970s it no longer seemed large enough or nice enough to continue to meet a governor's private and public needs. During these years it was sold, but the house still stands, just a stone's throw away from the current governor's mansion on Grand Avenue. In the earliest days, Grand Avenue was known as Adel Road, a dusty dirt road that was later paved and improved with sidewalks and guttering to become the gracious and important Grand Avenue that today is one of the busiest thoroughfares in Des Moines.

In 1971 the well-known and highly respected Hubbell family gave to the state Terrace Hill, the most famous and ornate house in Iowa, with the hope that it would be used as the governor's mansion. The house had been owned by the Hubbell family for eighty-seven years.

Terrace Hill is the legacy of two tycoons, Benjamin Franklin Allen and Frederick Hubbell. Each was an early Iowa settler who had moved to the Iowa region in his late teens; later, each of them made huge sums of money in land speculation, railroads, and insurance. Although both were founders of the Equitable Insurance Company, the two men were very different. Hubbell, ten years younger than Allen, was conservative and methodical—a speculator who quietly amassed a fortune that eventually surpassed that of Allen. Hubbell managed his risks, as contrasted with the flamboyant Allen, who was an impetuous businessman prone to spending sprees and careless investments.

Benjamin Allen had arrived in Iowa in 1848 as a nineteen-year-old speculator. He opened a general store and a sawmill, and he embarked on an ambitious land purchase program. "From 1848, when Polk County land transactions were first recorded in permanent volumes, until 1875 when Allen went bankrupt, he was involved in a minimum of 1,100 property purchases and sales in Polk County alone."[1] He was wildly successful before his eventual devastating failure in the banking business.

As the first Iowa millionaire and as testament to his great wealth, Allen built in 1867–1869 the twenty-room Terrace Hill mansion, spending an enormous sum—$250,000. This was at a time when most Des Moines houses were being built for less than $5,000. Cost was not a consideration for Allen, and he omitted no detail or embellishment. When workers began to clear a thirty-acre plot of ground for Allen to build his "prairie palace of the West,"[2] they had no way of knowing that in a few years, 1873, he would be on the verge of bankruptcy and that, over a hundred years later, his mansion would become the official residence of Iowa's governors.

Although Allen's Gilded Age fortune did not last, he had created an architectural legacy that would be preserved by his associate Frederick M. Hubbell. The glorious Terrace Hill would live on beyond both men and continue to serve Iowa into the future. In 1884, Hubbell, a bank attorney in Allen's bankruptcy case, bought many of Allen's assets, including the prized estate with its remaining eight acres, for a mere $60,000; in a futile effort to retain the house, Allen had earlier sold most of the acreage from the original parcel.

Terrace Hill was designed by the most famous Chicago architect of the time, William W. Boyington. The widely known nineteenth-century American architect had trained in New York before moving to Chicago in 1853. Originally a designer of public buildings such as railroad depots, hotels, and churches, Boyington's aesthetic sense bestowed grandeur and flourish to everyday structures. For example, he designed the Old Water Tower, a Gothic landmark and famous Chicago tourist attraction, to conceal a 138-foot-tall standpipe. In designing Terrace Hill, he visualized much more than a Second Empire style mansion: He laid out a lively nineteenth-century estate set in the middle of thirty acres that included a gardener's house, a greenhouse, a barn, and a coach house. There were orchards, vineyards, gravel paths, and formal gardens with exotic plants. J. T. Elletson, a landscape gardener whose resume included a stint at Buckingham

1. Scherrie Goettsch and Steve Weinberg, *Terrace Hill: The Story of a House and the People Who Touched It*, 11.
2. LeRoy G. Pratt, *Discovering Historic Iowa*, 206.

Palace, was brought in from New York. Today, this mansion is regarded as one of the country's finest examples of Second Empire–style architecture.

As the new owner, Hubbell installed a central heating system, thereby ending the total reliance on fireplaces for heat. He purchased a huge crystal chandelier for the main floor, and he is credited for commissioning the elaborate 9 x 11 foot stained-glass window that illuminates the stairway landing between the first and second floors. Hubbell reconfigured the third-floor ballroom to make sleeping quarters for his twelve servants. Today the third floor is the private living quarters for the governor's family.

During the next seventy-three years, three successive generations of Hubbells occupied Terrace Hill. Preserving and maintaining the house was an ongoing ritual of the Hubbell family, until 1957, when the last of the family moved from the house. Looked over by caretakers for the next several years, the house continued to be maintained, but without the day-to-day personal participation of the family.

For fourteen years the fate of Terrace Hill was unknown. Anna Hubbell, the last Hubbell to occupy it, and the other heirs were willing to arrange with the state of Iowa for it to acquire the mansion, but legislators were concerned that even if the mansion was entirely donated to the state, public ownership and maintenance of the building would be too expensive.

Robert Ray became governor in 1969, and a new day dawned for Terrace Hill. A bill was introduced in the legislature to explore again the state's acquisition of Terrace Hill. Discussions between Governor Ray and the Hubbell family began to show progress. Recognizing the need to replace the original governor's mansion, the legislature could no longer ignore the gift of Terrace Hill that was being placed on Iowa's doorstep.

When the Hubbells gave Terrace Hill and its eight surrounding acres to the state, Terrace Hill's tranquility as a privately owned house was replaced by a lively bustle in the transition to public ownership. In early photographs of the mansion's first floor, one notices that when Frederick Hubbell and Grover Hubbell lived there, the decor reflected self-confidence and inventiveness. The Hubbell House was formal but full of life. There were whimsical personal touches added by family members, many of which were mementos from family travels. During its later transformation to public ownership, the house became more serious and less eclectic—gone were the open-mouthed tiger rug and the antlers on the walls.

An estimated cost of $250,000 to convert the house to a governor's residence was found to be grossly inadequate. With the passage of time, consequent inflation, and the adoption of a more elaborate plan, the $250,000 estimate grew to $1.5 million.

The National Register of Historic Places announced in 1972 the inclusion of Terrace Hill as a historic site. This qualified Terrace Hill to receive federal funding for the restoration. Historic places included on the National Register qualify for grants but require local matching funds to be raised. The Terrace Hill Foundation therefore was created to take over the major fund-raising role. By 1989, three million dollars had been raised for the preservation of Terrace Hill.

Terrace Hill was built during an era of wealth, and its exquisite preservation and history have had an indelible effect on the people of Iowa. Despite the years of skepticism and debate about whether to appropriate, save, tear down, or move—or even whether to provide an official residence—the decision in favor of preservation of Terrace Hill illustrates historical continuity. Early concerns that the mansion might become a burden to the public were overcome thanks to the many public and private mansion groups working together as a partnership to serve the artistic and financial needs of the estate. These groups include the Terrace Hill Commission, the Terrace Hill Foundation, the Terrace Hill Society, and the Iowa State Questers. Elaine Estes, past president of the Terrace Hill Society Board of Directors and president of the Iowa State Questers, said it best: "the public-private partnership operates for the benefit of all and for this wonderful property."[3]

Over the years the carriage house was renovated to accommodate a tourist headquarters that includes a gift shop, classroom/reception area, offices, and a full workplace for staff and volunteers. Proceeds from the gift shop benefit the residence, and among the numerous souvenirs available are an extensive collection of Iowa and Terrace Hill history books.

By the year 2000, the caribou, elk, and moose trophy heads were restored and back on the walls. Their presence today evokes the bygone Victorian era and preserves a nuance of the Hubbell household. Dave Cordes, the administrator of Terrace Hill, concludes, "Trophy heads were a symbol of a certain kind of leisure travel. They were evidence of a wealthy gentleman's ability to afford extended hunting trips, and they were important decor in the well-to-do Victorian household."[4]

Terrace Hill is an ornate nineteenth-century landmark, "one of the finest examples of Victorian architecture in the Midwest."[5] Its old-fashioned refinement shows up in the quality of original workmanship. For example, the plaster arched doorways and coved ceilings are impeccably molded, and the pecan, chestnut, and oak wood mosaics on the floors are intricate and exquisitely patterned. The floors are complemented by rosewood stair rails and massive twelve-foot-high double doors. All of the doors are made from walnut, rosewood, and mahogany. Most of the first-floor rooms can be opened up to each other in order to expand their space, a technique frequently used in Victorian houses. The architect created a dramatic facade with two towers—one standing ninety feet tall—each with mansard roofs that look down on lower slate roofs and dormers. This contributes to the grandeur of the building and emphasizes its verticality.

In some ways Terrace Hill is like a museum of Victoriana. Its Second Empire style, imported from France, was widely adopted in America's Northeast and Midwest between 1855 and

3. Elaine Estes, interview by author, Des Moines, July 12, 1995, and telephone conversations with author, September 24, 2002.

4. David L. Cordes, interview by author, Des Moines, September 17, 2002.

5. Linda K. Thomson, "Terrace Hill: A Magnificent Gift to the State of Iowa," 903.

1885. Terrace Hill was built as a prime example of the popular Victorian era architecture whose characteristic mansard roof defines the Second Empire style. In the interior design, the walls, floors, windows, and furnishings are formal, evoking their Victorian roots. Original paint colors and stenciling on the walls and ceilings have been researched and restored. As one would expect in a Victorian house of such high style, gilding was popular, and the prevalent gold leafing shows up throughout the house. The first and second floors have fifteen-foot ceilings, and the first floor of the house has four thousand square feet of space. Victorian antiques are everywhere: Frederick Hubbell's favorite chair is in the library, and on the wall is a portrait print autographed by Queen Victoria. Furniture created by the master Victorian craftsman John Henry Belter is arranged in the rose-colored drawing room as it would have been during the middle 1800s. As G. E. Kidder Smith described it, "Terrace Hill is one of the few remaining masterpieces of its giddy era."[6]

Given the building's use for the governor's living quarters and a place for formal entertaining, a museum restoration would have been impractical. Rather, the place has been restored to respect and preserve the original design, while also allowing for a dynamic new life as a well-functioning governor's mansion.

Using early documentation, restorers have made the house and grounds look as they did in the Victorian era. As a luminous model of preservation, this historic landmark offers immediate gratification for visitors interested in architecture, period furniture, or simply in viewing a beautiful 135-year-old house that evokes a rich, colorful past.

6. G. E. Kidder Smith, *Source Book of American Architecture: 500 Notable Buildings from the 10th Century to the Present*, 240.

Terrace Hill, showing its elaborate towers.

Detail of side porches.

View of the front hall featuring Victorian-era furniture
and mounted elk and caribou trophy heads.

Side view of the house and a formal garden.

The drawing room with the famous Belter furniture.

Terrace Hill's grand staircase and stained-glass window.

Kansas
Governor's Mansion

National Register of Historic Places

Location: 1 Cedar Crest Road, Topeka

Construction Year: 1928

Cost: $60,000

Size: 5,890 square feet

Number of Rooms: 12

Architect: William D. Wight

Architectural Style: French Eclectic

Furniture Style: Country French and some antiques

In 1861, Topeka was picked for the capital of the new state of Kansas, and for the next forty years, twelve governors of Kansas lived in Topeka's hotels and boarding houses. Since 1901, however, Kansas has had two official governors' mansions. Cedar Crest is the well-known current governor's residence; the first governor's mansion was located downtown, at a site that is now a parking lot. Each in its own time has been the most prestigious house in the state, and their shared history includes the long debate and controversy that surrounded Cedar Crest's replacement of the older house.

Separated by more than forty years, two prominent Kansans built their dream houses. Neither could have foretold that his house would someday be linked with the other's in the history of Kansas, for each of their dream houses was destined to become an official Kansas governor's residence. Each building cost sixty thousand dollars, a huge sum in those days, and each was built as the epitome of the architectural trend of its era. The first was built in the city and played its prestigious role more than sixty years before the other house, which was built six miles away in the country.

As a new state, Kansas had a large debt and no money in its treasury. Its problems were greatly complicated by the outbreak of the Civil War. But by the 1880s, boom times had finally arrived in Kansas, and the wealthy citizens of Topeka were showing off their new prosperity by building large and expensive houses on Buchanan Street, just west of the center of town. One such man was Erasmus Bennett, a young horse breeder who also imported fine horses. He built a house in 1886 on a one-acre lot on the corner of Buchanan and Eighth Streets. It was referred to as "the horseman's villa" and said to be "the finest and most expensive house in Topeka at that time."[1]

Built to be a showplace in the Victorian era, when a mixture of architectural features was a popular theme, the Bennett House's architecture was a vigorous combination of styles. It had features that were Italian, Islamic, English Tudor, and Queen Anne. Old pictures confirm that the appearance of the house was like that of a small castle, "with lavish gingerbread trim of wooden lace."[2] There were turrets, a tower, and a third-floor promenade deck. Three-foot-tall initial monograms were etched into the glass of the double-entry doors. There were porticos, cupolas, and ornamental ironwork. The terra-cotta work was the first to be used in Topeka. The woodwork was hand polished by men brought in from the St. Louis Pullman works. Some of the inlaid floors and fine woodwork were of oak, others were of white pine, redwood, or sycamore. There was a hand-carved oak staircase. (The staircase, five of the fireplaces, and some of the woodwork would eventually be removed and, in 1965, installed in a new Ramada

1. Eileen Charbo, "Life in a Vanished Mansion," *Kansas City Times*, February 18, 1965, in "The Last Days of Our First Families' Home," *Topeka Capital Journal*, November 1, 1964; second quote from Hermione van Laer Adams, "The Governor's Mansion, 1901–1962," 5.

2. Kittie Dale, "Bennett Home: Kansas' First Executive Mansion," *Wichita Eagle-Beacon*, January 29, 1981.

Inn.) On the third floor the house contained a ballroom with a bandstand and a billiard room. The rococo red-brick mansion had seventy-five hundred square feet of living space and was designed by Seymour Davis, who later became the state architect.

Erasmus Bennett's horse sales were by invitation, and he attracted purchasers from all over the United States. His fine horses included Clydesdales, Percherons, Cleveland Bays, and French Coach horses. A small park in the middle of Eighth Street and next to the Bennett House served as a show ring for exhibiting the horses to prospective clients. According to old newspapers it was a familiar and enjoyable sight to see the grooms exercising the elegant horses on the unpaved streets.

For Erasmus Bennett, the close of the nineteenth century was an unstable financial time. Due to a national downturn in the economy that caused a decline in horse sales, he was forced to sell his mansion. The Bennett family sold the house to the state of Kansas in 1901 and moved to California. The state had finally decided to purchase a mansion for its governors and bought the house and its furnishings for $28,500, a superb value.

Between 1901 and 1962, twenty different governors lived in the "horseman's villa." As time progressed, the house began to show its age and despite basic maintenance the house continued to decline. Proposals began to come forth to modernize and renovate the mansion, but because of the cost, such work kept being postponed. Editorial writers and political reporters contributed their voices as to the condition of the mansion. In an article entitled "Mansion Rich in Legend, Short on Modern Comfort," the *Topeka State Journal* newspaper on July 26, 1951, reported that "Some day, somehow, in a burst of pride in the dignity of her highest office, Kansas will demand a home for her governors that will compare not unfavorably with the plush environment of a floor walker or an assistant receptionist of a funeral home."

Historically, most states at one time or another have been faced with a decision as to whether to attempt to maintain an old and sometimes historically important mansion, to build anew, or to move to an existing suitable structure. In Kansas, the outspoken media chipped away at the old building's appearance, undermining its status to such an extent that the public became aware that much more than painting and redecorating would be needed to correct it.

The incumbent governor, George Docking, and two former governors, Alf Landon and Fred Hall, advocated improving the existing house with extensive alterations. There were later governors, however, who would not live in the house, claiming it was shabby and too difficult to renovate. For many years the advocacy of Landon, Hall, and Docking for retaining the mansion prevailed over the detractors who were clamoring to tear it down.

It was the gift of a house to the state of Kansas that brought finality to the old Bennett House, ending its service as a governor's mansion. Frank MacLennan, owner and publisher of the *Topeka State Journal,* was an esteemed member of the Kansas civic community. MacLennan died in 1933; when his widow, Marge, died in 1955, she left their house—Cedar Crest—and 244 surrounding acres to the state.

Shortly after the MacLennan gift, the legislature voted to accept the gift of Cedar Crest to be used as an executive residence, despite the objections of Governor Docking, who was still in office at the time. He called Cedar Crest a "white elephant," refused to live in it, and insisted on remaining in the seventy-six-year-old Bennett House. In addition, Governor Docking tried, with no success, to influence the 1959 session of the Kansas legislature to relinquish title to Cedar Crest. In 1962, the new governor, John Anderson Jr., made Cedar Crest the official governor's residence. The legislature allocated a hundred thousand dollars to renovate the property so that it could more appropriately serve the needs of a governor. The Bennett House, an important historical building, was sold at auction for $28,500 in 1963. The buyers removed the interior fixtures that were later installed in the Ramada Inn, and the house was torn down in 1964 as part of a plan to construct an apartment building.

The MacLennan House has an interesting history. Forty-two years after Erasmus Bennett had constructed his house in the city, Frank MacLennan—who then owned a log cabin, used as a hunting lodge, on property that would one day become the site of the famed Menninger Clinic's chapel—began to think of building a larger retreat. He purchased a chunk of neighboring farmland, tore down the existing farm buildings, and began the construction of Cedar Crest. The year was 1928, and the national trend was for wealthy families to build and live on large country estates, removed from the activity of the city.

William D. Wight, a prominent architect from Kansas City, designed and built a manor house of buff-colored stucco and stone. The architectural style of the house was French Eclectic, designed to resemble country houses found in the Normandy province of France. These houses tend to vary, and their architecture has much in common with Tudor style and English traditions. This particular example of the French Eclectic style of architecture is formal and symmetrical. It has casement windows, a slate roof, and thick brick, stone, and stucco walls. Because the front of the house also has a tall round tower with a conical roof, it is identified as an example of the subtype called "towered French Eclectic."[3] MacLennan named the house Cedar Crest because of its location at the crest of a hill overlooking the Kansas River Valley, which is filled with cedars.

MacLennan's house reflects his Scottish ancestry and his publishing career. For example, he embellished it with decorative renderings of both thistle and printer's bookplates. Thistle, a Scottish emblem, is carved in the stone pediment above the front door, is incorporated into the stained-glass windows at the top of the staircase, and even appears on the gutter downspouts. The thistle motif as well as early trademarks of European printers dating to 1457 are carved into various places in the study. Displaying his love for the printed word, MacLennan had bookplates of his favorite authors painted on the walls of his study.

Marge MacLennan's gift to the state served to perpetuate her husband's memory. She left the house and its 244 acres with the proviso that part of the acreage be used as the grounds adjoin-

3. Virginia McAlester and Lee McAlester, *Field Guide to America's Historic Neighborhoods and Museum Houses* 364.

ing the governor's mansion and the remainder become a public park to be known as MacLennan Park. At the time of the gift to the state, Cedar Crest and its grounds were valued at two hundred thousand dollars.

By 1975, when Robert Bennett (no relation to Erasmus Bennett) became governor, pressure had accumulated from various quarters to tear down Cedar Crest and start afresh with a new building. The Bennetts felt that the charm of Cedar Crest could not be replicated. Their arguments were ironically similar to those advanced twenty years earlier, when Governor Docking had argued to continue using the original mansion and urged the legislature to reject the Cedar Crest gift.

Governor Bennett prevailed, however, and the legislature appropriated a hundred thousand dollars for a huge renovation of the fifty-year-old house. The project entailed replacing wiring and plumbing, adding insulation, repainting, and putting in new carpeting. The original plaster of the dining-room ceiling had been designed and molded to depict grapes, primrose, pears, vines, and Scottish thistle. At an earlier time the ceiling had been repainted in white. Recognizing the importance of the original work, Olivia Bennett, the governor's wife, hired the Kansas artist Paige Clark, who painted the ceiling, restoring it to its original look.

John W. Carlin defeated Governor Bennett in 1978 and served two four-year terms as governor. Karen Carlin, his second wife, was instrumental in the establishment of the Friends of Cedar Crest Association, a not-for-profit statewide organization that assists the first family in an advisory capacity. The association oversees the maintenance of the mansion and its furnishings and helps with some of the fund-raising activities.

Cedar Crest is included in both the Kansas State Register of Historic Places and the National Register of Historic Places. As a result of the work of the Friends of Cedar Crest, the mansion looked better and brighter. They removed wall-to-wall carpeting from the first floor, exposing the original stunning oak and walnut pegged floors in both the living room and the entry hall. In the dining room and sun room, the beautiful oak parquet floors were also refinished to a perfect sheen. Thus the mansion floors were returned to their original 1928 look.

Governor Mike Hayden, in office from 1987 to 1991, expressed his lifelong interest in wildlife and the outdoors by completing the development of MacLennan Park. He encouraged wildlife, increased vegetation, and built hiking and jogging trails. Although his efforts made the outdoor park area a place of distinction, public access to the park encroached on the privacy of the governor's family. People reached it by way of a parking lot adjoining the Cedar Crest driveway.

Governor Bill Graves served two terms beginning in 1994. During his tenure, his wife, Linda, led a statewide effort to raise $4.4 million to restore Cedar Crest. The legislature appropriated $2.2 million, and Linda Graves raised the remaining half from private sources. As lovely as the house was, it still did not live up to its potential until the eighteen-month renovation restored infrastructure, enlarged certain areas, and polished up the interior. One of the first accomplishments was installation of a security fence built around the residence grounds and separating the governor's residence from the public parking lot. The sunflower is the Kansas state flower, and large copper and iron sunflowers adorn the beautiful gates. The iron fence and gates are proportionately appropriate for the property and look as if they have always been there.

This most recent renovation of Cedar Crest, managed by Jennie Adams Rose, was completed in the year 2000. In this state-of-the-art restoration, much of the infrastructure was replaced. The heating and air-conditioning had been linked in such a way that they ran at the same time, and this problem was rectified. Additionally, lead pipes were replaced and asbestos was removed throughout. Most of this work was behind the walls, but visible changes were made as well. Although some furnishings were replaced with the Country French style, to better complement the French-inspired architecture, those furnishings that were historically significant to this or the first governor's residence were retained for use in Cedar Crest. A new entrance was created from the dining room to an outside patio. The outdoor stone patios were enlarged to almost surround the house, in order to accommodate large outdoor events.

Cedar Crest, a solidly built house in the European country tradition, sits atop a bluff on the western edge of Topeka, overlooking the Kansas River valley. When seen from a distance, Cedar Crest looks like a true French chateau in the middle of a forest. First Lady Linda Graves frequently expressed her enthusiasm for the country setting: "It is so appropriate that in Kansas, the governor's residence is not in the shadow of the Capitol, but is instead located in a more pastoral setting."

The park, with its dense forests and rugged outdoor demeanor, in one sense contrasts with the calm tranquility of the mansion, but the landscaping around the mansion tastefully blends its architecture with the surrounding MacLennan Park. As both a showplace for the great natural beauty of Kansas and as a home for the state's chief executive, Cedar Crest fulfills its purpose with dignity and charm.

Dining room with original plaster ceiling work of fruit, vines, and Scottish thistle.

Full front facade of Cedar Crest.

Exterior side view, featuring exterior chimney with decorative chimney pot.

Living room with stone fireplace, beautiful woods, and bookcases.

Location: 2520 Oxford Road, Lansing

Construction Year: 1959

Cost: $50,000–70,000 (estimated)*

Size: 10,300 square feet

Number of Rooms: 12

Architect: Wallace Frost

Architectural Style: Ranch

Furniture Style: Transitional

Michigan
Governor's Mansion

Summer Residence

National Register of Historic Places

Location: Fort Street, Mackinac Island

Construction Year: 1902

Cost: $15,000

Size: 7,104 square feet

Number of Rooms: 24

Architect: Frederick W. Perkins

Architectural Style: Shingle style

Furniture Style: Victorian-style wicker
   and maple antiques

* Estimated price, based on sales prices of houses in
the same area sold in 1959; actual cost not available.

When in 1701, Antoine Cadillac, a French soldier and fur trader, established a small trading post on the eastern shore of what is now the state of Michigan, he could not foresee that one day this settlement would grow into one of the largest and most important cities on the North American continent—a major industrial manufacturing center—the city of Detroit. His legacy would give rise to the automobile capital of the world, would transform Michigan from an agricultural state to an industrial one, and cause a mass migration from farms to cities. Not only did the automobile headquarters and its outpouring of products outshine Monsieur Cadillac's own grand economic dreams, but these products changed forever the culture of America and of the whole industrialized world.

Michigan is the biggest state in the Midwest; together, its two peninsulas and their surrounding waters form the region's prime vacation land. The Lower Peninsula holds most of the state's population, the capital city of Lansing, as well as the manufacturing metropolis of Detroit. The Upper Peninsula, bounded on the north by Lake Superior and mostly surrounded by water, is the principal recreation center. Upper Michigan's most famous place is Mackinac Island, which is the summer home of the Michigan governors. Michigan is the only state in the Midwest with two governors' residences.

The Michigan area was included in the old Northwest Territory, but by 1805 it had achieved an identity of its own and was recognized as the Michigan Territory, although the boundaries of the territory changed frequently. The area's population grew rapidly, and huge fortunes were made in the fur trade; prosperity was also fueled by the rich timberlands and through successful farming of the fertile soil. Good roads were laid, steamboats were built, and the Erie Canal was opened in 1825, providing a safe water transportation link between the Hudson River and the Great Lakes. Easterners began pouring into Michigan via the new water route "which made travel time from Detroit to New York one-tenth of what it had been."[1]

In 1837 Michigan became the twenty-sixth state to join the Union. Detroit, as the capital of the territorial government, became the temporary seat of the new state's government, but the state constitution stipulated that the legislature should permanently locate the capital by 1847. Fierce competition fueled controversy over where to place the capital. There was a stalemate between those who wanted to leave the capital in Detroit and those who wished to relocate it to an existing town. A tangle of unnamed forest, later named Lansing, was chosen as a compromise, principally because it was located centrally in the Lower Peninsula. Another favorable condition for its selection was its potential as a new town to attract new settlement and create new opportunities for speculation.

For the next hundred years, Michigan provided no residence for its governors. The idea was considered from time to time, but nothing came of it. In 1849 a small frame house near the capitol was being readied as a residence for third-term returning governor John S. Barry, a wealthy merchant. Governor Barry complained about the house being too small, forcing upon him an unacceptably lower living standard from that to which he was accustomed. He pre-

---

1. Suzanne Winckler, *The Great Lakes States,* 320.

ferred to commute to Lansing from his home in Constantine and to rent a temporary apartment while the legislature was in session.

Governor's residence considerations were suspended until 1879, when former governor Austin Blair urged that governors of the state should be provided with a house. He complained about living in a hotel during his tenure as governor during the Civil War. In 1903 Governor Aaron Bliss reopened the discussions. But despite years of complaints, no action was taken until 1945, when the state spent fifteen thousand dollars to purchase a home on Mackinac Island as a summer residence for its governors.

Earnest discussions were under way by 1947 to address the lack of an official, year-round governor's residence. The proposal of a local architect to build a house costing $250,000 might have been accepted, but reports from the press alerted the public that the plan included a fish pond that would extend from outside to inside the house, making the proposal seem extravagant and undeserving of serious consideration.

In 1948 a Victorian manse situated near the capitol and overflowing with history and architectural charm was offered to the state of Michigan as a home for its governors. Although Governor Kim Sigler exerted his influence, lobbying the state to accept the gift, he was unable to convince the legislature to spend the estimated two hundred thousand dollars required to make the house liveable, and thus it never was used as a governor's residence.

While Michigan was the first and only state in the Midwest to provide a summer mansion for its governors, it was the last state in the region to provide them a year-round residence. Not having a residence in Lansing presented a major inconvenience for governors and their families. Many important guests to the capital were required to stay in hotels or in homes of friends of the governor. But the general feeling among legislators was that the purchase of a governor's residence was too expensive and that the state had more important priorities.

In 1955, when Governor G. Mennen (Soapy) Williams was in the middle of his long tenure, two young legislators sponsored a bill to appropriate $10,000 from the state, with the condition that an additional $250,000 or so be raised from individuals and corporations in the private sector, to provide for the acquisition of a permanent governor's mansion. A commission was appointed, a study was made, but, before the legislators could agree on where the money should come from, they became embroiled in a tax fight, and the governor's residence plans were again shelved.

In 1968 Michigan received a free governor's mansion. The trucking executive Howard Sober offered his twelve-room house without charge to the state, although he requested $250,000 for the interior furnishings, which he said consisted of antiques, fine art, and furniture specially made to complement the house. The cost of the furnishings was to be paid for by private fundraising, which helped to offset possible legislative objections about accepting Sober's gift.

The popular Governor George W. Romney was then nearing the end of his gubernatorial term, and after touring the house he pronounced it ideally fit with the state and recommended acceptance of the gift. Thus, after a century of discussion, with Romney's endorsement and the prospect of no state funds being required, legislative approval was obtained. Michigan finally owned a governor's residence located in its capital city.

But praise turned to criticism when the private fund-raising failed to work out. Ten prominent citizens had temporarily assumed the debt, and when legislation was passed to reimburse them from public money, complaints about the cost of the furniture multiplied. Some legislators and the press claimed the furniture was overvalued and did not justify the high price.

The newspaper accounts of the controversy would cause anyone to be curious to see the inside of this house. Although the residence is not open to the public at the present time, it is occasionally featured on a special house or garden tour.

The governor's residence is on Oxford Road in the Moores River Drive area of Lansing—an area of quiet, tree-lined streets bordering the Grand River and the Country Club of Lansing. Started in the 1920s as an exclusive subdivision, it is now fully developed and continues to be considered quite a desirable residential area in Lansing.

Built in 1959 for Letha and Howard Sober, the house is an expansive, L-shaped, modern, 1950s ranch. As such it is a residential example of that era's contemporary architecture. Michigan architect Wallace Frost designed the house. Early in Frost's career he had worked for famed architect Albert Kahn, who was known for his modern innovative design of commercial buildings. Prior to his work with Kahn, Frost was trained in classical architecture, and it was a mixture of classical and modern innovative styles that he brought to the design of the Sober House. Frost's classical background presents itself in the house's balance and sense of proportion. The house is not considered avant-garde or extreme, but its horizontal lines, curved walls, and multiple glass windows give it a definite contemporary character.

The one-story house has a beautiful setting on three acres of well-landscaped grounds overlooking the Grand River. The outdoors area is a great attribute of this house. Emphasizing natural elements, it contains attractive gardens and terraces made of Ohio bluestone. In the warmer season it can be used as an outdoor room. The facade of the house is rock and painted brick, with a limestone-framed entrance and a wood-paneled door.

The foyer of the house is dramatic: Its buff-colored Italian marble floor is elevated three steps above the living room, and it forms a semicircle around the living room and dining room. The effect is of being on a stage with the living room on one side and a curved wall of gorgeous, champagne-colored wood paneling on the other. But the paneling is not really a wall; some of the sections open separately to reveal closets. This functionalism is typical of modern houses built in the 1950s and 1960s.

Standing in the foyer and viewing the living room below and beyond, one sees a wall of windows looking out onto the garden. On each side of the steps leading down to the living room are large built-in rectangular marble planters—the smaller one is six and a half feet long and the larger is fifteen feet long. The large living room has a fifteen-foot-high ceiling and leads to the oval dining room, which has a wall of windows looking out to the gardens and walkways. Adjacent to the dining room is the garden room, which connects the house to the outside patio.

This casual house was designed with every convenience known in the 1950s. Reflecting an era intrigued with gadgets and electronic conveniences, it featured such motorized accessories as push-button-controlled living-room drapes and a built-in motorized bar that looks like a curved wall when closed and opens to be a room for the bartender. As was also typical of the times, there was special-effect lighting and a master stereo system. During the administration of the first governor's family to occupy the house, Governor and Mrs. William Milliken, the power unit for the motor-driven drapes failed and was converted to manual operation.

The house has 10,300 square feet of living space, and most of it is light and bright. It is open and informal and provides an easy, comfortable, and cheerful place in which to live. In terms of a governor's residence, the physical drawback to the house is its lack of space for large sit-down dinners. But conversely it is well designed for large receptions. Indeed, the original owners used the house for cocktail party entertaining, and the open flow of the house enables traffic to move with ease from space to space and, in nice weather, to the outside gardens and patios.

From the beginning, some of the furnishings in the house were considered odd for a governor's residence—things like a rock crystal chandelier Sober claimed cost twelve thousand dollars and the abovementioned bar room operated by push button. This fifties-style bar, prominently placed between the foyer and the living room, inspired whimsical description. For example, the *Detroit Free Press* told its readers that, "If anything, the house is reminiscent of a Hollywood set filled with costly furnishings collected from the films of stars like Jean Harlow (early), Robert Taylor and Joan Crawford."[2]

Since the state took over the Sober House in 1969, the look of the furnishings has changed. The eclectic mix of furniture from the Sober days was initially modified and redefined. Some of it was rather unstable, and some first ladies thought Oriental or French styles did not fit well with the style of the house. As time passed, the furniture was gradually replaced, so that now only the dining-room chandelier remains. The residence is now furnished in a comfortable transitional style that fits the interior as well as the exterior environment. Funding for the purchase and updating of furnishings was procured through the establishment of the Friends of the Governor's Residence in 1985 and the Oxford Foundation in the 1990s.

Truly, a great benefit for Michigan and its governors is the three-story, twenty-four-room, Shingle-style Mackinac Island summer house that the state acquired in 1945. The state purchased the property for its original 1902 cost of fifteen thousand dollars. The house is a historic beauty. Although terribly run down at the time of purchase, it was immediately restored and renovated using the labor of prison inmates.

Governor Harry F. Kelly was the first governor to occupy the Mackinac mansion. Prior to the purchase of the Mackinac residence, several residences, built in the 1870s for officers of old Fort Mackinac, were used by governors during the summer months. That fact caused Mackinac Island to become known as "Michigan's summer capital." Recognizing this tradition, the legislature in 1935 directed the Mackinac Island State Park Commission to find a home on the island for the governor's use. The house that had been the commander's of Fort Mackinac was then set aside for the governor. This was an informal and temporary arrangement. W. F. Doyle, dean

2. *Detroit Free Press*, December 11, 1972.

of the Mackinac Island State Park Commission and Lansing lobbyist, had his eye on a property owned by Mrs. Hugo Scherer of Grosse Pointe. The house, built in 1902 by one of the early developers of Mackinac, was purchased by Mrs. Scherer in 1924. She rarely used it, and when she eventually agreed to sell it to the state, Doyle was ready with a fifteen-thousand-dollar appropriation. Because he knew the conservative, largely rural legislature would not look upon an official summer residence for the governor as a necessity, Doyle made sure the enabling legislation did not contain the words *governor's mansion*. It merely directed the appropriated money to the commission for the purchase of additional land. As previously stated, the price the state paid for the house was the same as the original 1902 cost to build the house.

The summer governor's residence is situated on a rocky bluff overlooking the Straits of Mackinac. It was designed in 1902 by a Chicago architect named Frederick Perkins and was constructed by Patrick Doud and his crew of Mackinac Islanders, who built many of the large summer houses there. The Victorian Shingle style of architecture used throughout Mackinac makes these houses similar to those in other U.S. resorts of that era. Oversized limestone chimneys complement the limestone boulders used in the house's foundation and provide natural embellishment to the house. The cottage has eleven bedrooms and eight bathrooms. When the house was constructed, its native pine shingle exterior was stained dark, as were many of the Shingle-style houses on the bluffs, but most of them are now white, as is the governor's residence.

In contrast to the white of the exterior, including the veranda, the house's balustrades, and its white picket fence, the cozy interiors are natural wood that has mellowed to dark. The interior is walnut and imported yellow pine paneling. There is wicker furniture covered in bright colors and Victorian-type furniture casually mixed with comfortable overstuffed chairs and fat sofas. The effect is an understated, homey appearance.

It is easy to see why the summer residence, so eloquently built into the environment, is often referred to as "Michigan's front porch." The view from the veranda, which wraps around three sides of the house, is said to be the best in Mackinac. This panoramic vista, framed by the large, graceful fir trees near the cottage, takes in the Mackinac harbor and shipping channel, the nearby Straits of Mackinac, and the famous Mackinac Bridge, connecting Michigan's two peninsulas.

Affording a change of pace for the governors of Michigan has proven beneficial to the state. The governor's summer home has brought a long list of dignitaries to Mackinac Island, including governors of other states, senators, presidential hopefuls, and presidents. A great deal of media publicity has surrounded these occasions, publicizing the beauty and history of Mackinac Island to the country at large. The Mackinac house is open for tours during the summer season and attracts many visitors—in fact the quaint island is a mecca for tourists from all over. Mackinac Island maintains a sense of the nineteenth century with its many rambling Victorian houses (called "cottages," although they often have ten to twenty or more rooms), its exclusion of automobiles from the island, and its horsedrawn buggies that carry people on its streets. The summer governor's mansion is enhanced by the romantic setting of Mackinac, while the mansion itself adorns the island with prestige and a simple grace.

This backyard gathering place becomes an outdoor room in summer.

Living room with marble planters that are changed seasonally.

Summer governor's residence, showing limestone-boulder
foundation and chimneys. *Photograph by Peter Medler.*

Dining-room table setting.

Minnesota
Governor's Mansion

National Register of Historic Places

Location: 1006 Summit Avenue, St. Paul

Construction Year: 1912

Cost: $50,000

Size: 15,340 square feet

Number of Rooms: 20

Architect: William Channing Whitney

Architectural Style: Beaux Arts English Tudor

Furniture Style: European antiques and reproductions

The land occupied by Minnesota was handed from country to country as part of the spoils of wars for almost two hundred years. The land has been owned by four different nations—twice by France and, in between, by Spain and Britain. In 1803 France sold it to the United States as part of the Louisiana Purchase. Today it is almost as if the homogeneity of Minnesota's large Scandinavian and German population was purposely calculated to offset the state's restless history.

Minnesota became an official territory in 1849, and at that time the village of St. Paul became its capital. Thus the capital city of Minnesota has a long history as a place for affluent and influential people and dignified architecture. The historian Ernest R. Sandeen described St. Paul's Summit Avenue, one of the town's most historic neighborhoods, as "the best preserved American example of the Victorian monumental residential boulevard."[1]

St. Paul's Summit Avenue, and the Minnesota governor's residence, which is on it, do not disappoint. Summit Avenue is on a bluff overlooking the Mississippi River and downtown St. Paul. The wharf area below was the hub of the city in the old days, the place where fur traders made their living. By 1850, St. Paul's river port was bursting with energy and commercial activity. Boatloads of settlers flooded the wharves, and, as the population outgrew the riverbank, well-to-do citizens began to build houses on the bluffs above.

Summit Avenue is a historic residential area built largely in the latter part of the nineteenth century, employing architectural models from several earlier periods. In its early years it truly was an enclave of privilege for the prospering industrialists of St. Paul, people who could hire prominent architects to design landmark architecture for their huge houses. One of these architects was a popular practitioner of the Beaux Arts style, Cass Gilbert, who lived in St. Paul for a number of years.

Situated on four and a half miles of bluff whose terraced hillside descends to the Mississippi River, Summit Avenue has held on to the atmosphere of a bygone era. It is a wide boulevard, lined by trees. What was once a grassy bridle path in the center is today landscaped with shrubbery, contributing to the parklike atmosphere of the street. Houses built of stone and brick, designed in the popular architectural styles of the day, make liberal use of ironwork, stained glass, and marble. Ongoing preservation has largely maintained this boulevard as it once was, thereby retaining an important part of St. Paul history. In 1954, future Supreme Court justice Warren Burger sued the city to prevent his neighbor from changing his residence to a fourplex. The Minnesota Supreme Court ruled in his favor, thereby striking down a 1943 amendment and reenforcing a 1915 zoning law that prevents residents from converting to multiple dwellings.

The largest house ever built on Summit was begun in 1887 and completed in 1891. It is the thirty-five-room, four-story Romanesque home of James J. Hill, who had amassed a fortune as the owner of one of the great American railroad empires, the Great Northern–Northern Pacific–Burlington system. Hill's most celebrated achievement was completing the Great

1. Ernest R. Sandeen, *St. Paul's Historic Summit Avenue*, 1.

Northern Railway between St. Paul and Puget Sound. He built a thirty-six-thousand-square-foot house that looks like an Elizabethan castle; it was the largest house in the Midwest when it was constructed, and it remains the largest house on Summit. Across the street from it, Hill helped to build the Cathedral of St. Paul, the eastern anchor of Summit Avenue.

Quieter, smaller and less dramatic is the house that was built at 1006 Summit in 1911–1912 by the lumber baron Horace Hills Irvine. The prosperous Irvine, who inherited his stake in the lumber business from his father, was also a lawyer as well as a founder of Northwest Airlines. Irvine hired architect William Channing Whitney, who had previously studied under the prominent architect Cass Gilbert. Whitney designed the Irvine House as a Beaux Arts interpretation of a Tudor manor house.

Today there are 373 houses on Summit, but when Irvine built his estate, which is now the governor's residence, there were fewer than two hundred Summit Avenue houses. The Eclectic movement lasted from 1889 to about 1940, peaking in popularity between 1890 and 1917; the Eclectic style houses built during the peak were large, expensive, and wrapped in formality. Like the Irvine House, they were usually built of masonry and festooned with carvings and classical ornamentation. Embracing everything from Period house styles to Modern house styles, and inspired by historic European houses, Eclectic houses do not fit into a specific category because they are always an interpretation of two or more house styles that have been combined. The details of the various designs were copied with great accuracy, but it was the combination of styles that produced Eclecticism. Now, as then, Summit is a place where a showy array of architectural styles exists.

The Irvine House is a formal English Tudor house that employs Beaux Arts elements to add balance and symmetry to the exterior. One example is seen in the building's shape; a conventional Tudor house would have had an asymmetrical shape, but this Beaux Arts adaptation is rectangular and balanced.

The architect, Whitney, reinforced the Tudor appearance by using very dark brick for the house's facade. True to its Tudor style, there are steeply pitched roofs and multiple chimneys. The steep gables have limestone edging and parapets that extend above the roofline. They give the house a formal look, reminiscent of the walls surrounding the balcony or roof of a fortress.

Constructed in two years at a cost of fifty thousand dollars, the completed 15,340-square-foot house contains more than twenty rooms, nine fireplaces, and even a separate dining room for the live-in servants of the original owners. The house accommodated the six members of the Irvine family as well as the household help that, at times, numbered seven.

Horace Irvine lived in the house with his family until his death in 1947. When his widow, Clotilde, died, the family had lived in the house fifty-two years. In 1965, the Irvine daughters gave the house to the state of Minnesota to use as a residence for its governors. For the 107 years between statehood and the Irvine gift, Minnesota governors had been forced to find their own places to live. State Representative William J. O'Brien, a longtime proponent of the acquisition of an official house for the governor, was instrumental in the state's acceptance of the property. In 1965, while a member of the Minnesota House of Representatives and president of his family's charitable foundation, the Alice O'Brien Family Foundation, he and the other principals purchased the double lot adjoining the residence and gave it to the state. Used for parking and for enlarging the residence grounds, this addition gave the house a more gracious setting and a larger presence. At this time, the governor's mansion's official name became the State Ceremonial Building.

Approaching the house, one passes through iron gates topped by a decorative wrought-iron overhead arch displaying the house number. Following the sidewalk to the house, one is able to look up and see the outline of gables and parapets against the slate roof. Below the roofline are window bays separated by vertical stone mullions. The Beaux Arts influence becomes apparent in the stone columns on either side of the entrance and the stone quoins that accentuate the corners of the brick exterior. The short terrace area extending across the front entrance is bordered by a stone balustrade.

The arched entrance to the residence provides a covered shelter with massive double doors and wrought-iron grillwork. The front vestibule opens, with a second set of double doors—these being leaded glass—into a large, square foyer or great hall similar to those found in English manor houses two centuries ago. This room features an antique grandfather clock that was made in Scotland and came to St. Paul by steamboat. The clock has a silver dial and a cherry case, but its date of origin is unknown. The great hall also contains two armchairs dating from 1850, which were originally owned by the Earl of Derby, England. These chairs were originally upholstered in ostrich skin; the upholstery has been changed, but the beautiful inlaid wood of floral design and the brass finial knobs attest to the remarkable antique quality of the chairs.

The main staircase leads from the grand hall to a landing, where a window seat encourages one to ponder the scene beyond the front bay windows positioned above the entry doors. Overlooking this landing is a beautiful 1929 portrait of Horace H. Irvine's daughter Elizabeth Hills Irvine, at age twenty, dressed for her coming-out party.

Back on the first floor, the great hall also leads to the library and other rooms. When visiting this house, with its emphasis on interior woods, one understands how deep is the legacy of this lumberman. For example, the walls of the foyer are of golden oak, those of the living room are of dark African mahogany, and those of the dining room are Circassian walnut. Various woods appear throughout the building in the form of mantles, molding, beams, wainscoting, finials, and staircases.

The small and cozy library had been Olivia Irvine Dodge's favorite room. It is easy to see why she, the youngest of the Irvine children, would like it: The room is charming and elegant, its walls paneled halfway in oak, with the upper half of rough plaster and the ceiling of decorative wood and plaster. A stone fireplace with an oak mantle, flanked by tall bookcases, covers one wall. On the front wall is a bay with a series of windows providing both light and a view. When the Irvines were not entertaining, the library was the room the family used the most. Every evening before dinner, the Irvine family gathered in the library for canapes; after dinner, they returned to it to listen to the radio. At every other time, it was—and still is—the kind of room where one would want to read, listen to music, or tell stories. Now there are ceremonial flags in front of the bookcases; this is the room we see on television when current governors give press conferences.

The second and third floors of the house have nine bedrooms, and in the old days there were sleeping porches, a sewing room, and a room on the third floor that was referred to as a ballroom; it was sometimes used for parties, though the architect had labeled it simply as an "open attic." That space is now used for storage, and the other second- and third-floor spaces have been reconfigured to accommodate a different lifestyle; today they comprise the private living quarters available for the governor.

When the Minnesota legislature accepted the Irvine gift, it appropriated money to transform the house from a private residence to a governor's residence. The building was still in the midst of renovation in 1967 when Governor and Mrs. Harold LeVander became the second gubernatorial family to occupy the house, and it became evident that an additional appropriation was needed, bringing the total cost of the conversion to $330,000.

This massive renovation included interior decoration as well as exterior work and landscaping. To enhance the landscape, Mrs. LeVander promoted a means of publicly recognizing the bravery of Minnesota soldiers during the Vietnam War. In 1970 Paul T. Granlund, a Minnesota artist, created a sculpture to sit on the front lawn of the residence. This memorial is now an important sculpture on the mansion's grounds, and it showcases wildflowers and trees native to Minnesota.

The governor's residence was included in the National Register of Historic Places in 1974, and in 1976 it was again put on the National Register when it was included with a portion of Summit Avenue that was placed on the register as a district. In 1978, the house was listed on St. Paul's Historic Sites Register by the city's Heritage Preservation Commission.

Minnesota's State Ceremonial Building Council oversees and manages fund-raising and restoration activities for the residence, and another nonprofit volunteer group, the 1006 Summit Avenue Society, has published cookbooks to raise money for the house.

A children's garden was added to the backyard of the residence by Governor and Mrs. Arne Carlson, who lived in the house from 1991 until 1998. Flagstone and gravel paths intersect the flower beds, and a lily pond wanders through the space; engraved on plaques throughout the garden are the names of children who have lived in the house.

Despite the generous overall use of wood, the Minnesota governor's residence remains cheerful and does not impart a "heavy" feeling. The specialized carving on the heavily paneled interiors of this house is detailed, elaborate, and delicate. Decorative wall and ceiling moldings gracefully curve, and the wood paneling is so lustrous that it almost glows. These interiors reflect the vitality of the lumber milling industry that was at its peak about the time the house was built.

The reproductions and fine antiques used in the house are solid, warm, and comfortable. The Irvine family had donated some of the antique furniture to the house. In the living room there is an ornately carved seventeenth-century oak chest, and in the solarium is a Jacobean refractory table and an old Steinway piano that are original to the house.

The porchlike solarium is bright and airy, with many French doors and windows. This room differs in style from the other first-floor rooms in that it has gray marble floors and stone walls instead of wood. Opening to the outside patio, it provides the transition linking the formal rooms of the first floor with the gardens and the informal outdoor environment.

Once a family home on the outskirts of St. Paul, this gift of the Irvine family has, over the last third of a century, provided a home to eight governors' families. These families have maintained the residence in a manner appropriate to the Irvines' intentions. Throughout the years, the occupants of the house have practiced preservation. The richly polished woods have not been allowed to crack and dry, nor have redecoration or renovation plans been permitted to violate the past. The architecture, provenance, and even the neighborhood in which it resides retain and preserve an old-fashioned atmosphere reminding us of the culture of old St. Paul, yet the mansion today maintains its grace and is able to fulfill the modern housing needs of each governor.

Minnesota governor's residence, front angle.

Golden oak staircase seen from the great hall, showing
Elizabeth Hills Irvine's portrait in the background.

Drawing room of dark mahogany walls
and ornately carved mantel surroundings
and the marble fireplace.

Front facade featuring wrought-iron arch and stone pillars.

The library was said to be the Irvine family's most-used room. This is where Governor Jesse Ventura held televised press conferences.

Missouri
Governor's Mansion

National Register of Historic Places

Location: 100 Madison Street, Jefferson City

Construction Year: 1871

Cost: $75,000 (including furnishings)

Size: 18,290 square feet

Number of Rooms: 22

Architect: George Ingram Barnett

Architectural Style: Italian and French Renaissance

Furniture Style: Renaissance Revival

Missouri was originally settled by the French and was part of the vast area known as the Louisiana Territory. In 1803, when Napoleon Bonaparte sold that territory to the United States, several of the communities in present-day Missouri had already been established, including Ste. Genevieve, St. Louis, and St. Charles.

The enormous Louisiana Territory was divided by Congress into two sections, each having its own governor, one in New Orleans and one in St. Louis. The Missouri of today was not officially separated and identified—as the Missouri Territory—until 1812.

During Missouri's territorial years, the state capital was located in St. Charles. In 1821, when Congress granted statehood to Missouri, the Missouri legislature appointed five commissioners from different parts of the state to begin searching for a more centrally located site for the new state's capital. They chose a bluff in the middle of the state, situated on the south side of the Missouri River. It was high enough above the river to be safe from floods, while still close enough to the river to use it for the transportation of goods and services. At the time the city was founded, the only resident was a barkeeper who sold whiskey to passing boatmen. Twenty years earlier, however, Lewis and Clark had rested on this land on their way to explore the West. The spot chosen by the commissioners was named the City of Jefferson in honor of the third president of the United States, who had brought Missouri into the Union through his purchase of the Louisiana Territory.

By 1826, the first official government building had been constructed in Jefferson City, and it served as both a capitol building and a residence for the governor. Built of brick and containing ten rooms, the building's dual function provided only limited accommodations for family life. It housed the legislature on the first and second floors, leaving only two rooms per floor for living quarters. In order to provide better accommodations for a governor and his family, five thousand dollars was appropriated by the legislature in 1832 for a separate governor's residence. This two-story building, constructed from local limestone, was completed in 1834 and was located adjacent to the first capitol/residence building, which then became the capitol building only.

The new building was satisfactory for a time, but eventually governors occupying the new house complained that it was too small for entertaining and living. The feeling was that the grounds should be expanded and the living quarters of the house should be made less public, and more like a private home. Entertaining in the governor's residence was limited by the size of the public rooms, which accommodated a maximum of a hundred people. Large groups like the legislature had to be broken into smaller parties for separate entertaining. By 1840, Jefferson City had grown to hold a population of over one thousand people, and the governor's mansion was the center of social activity.

Almost every governor between 1844 and 1871 lobbied the legislature for funds to build a bigger, more accommodating mansion. An allocation was actually promised in 1861, but the outbreak of the Civil War caused the project to be abandoned.

By 1871, only six years after the end of the Civil War, Jefferson City was a growing, industrious community of five thousand, having a largely German population. The town had progressed far beyond its earlier rough frontierism. Its citizens wanted to improve Jefferson City's image to demonstrate that the hostility and tensions of the war had been overcome. Missouri had been a border state during the Civil War and the site of several battles in which Missourians fought on both the Confederate and Union sides. The state had undergone major industrial changes and progressed from war-torn chaos to a new peacefulness and prosperity. There was a new sense of community among its citizens.

When Governor B. Gratz Brown took office as the nineteenth governor of the Missouri, many of the state's residents refused to attend his reception in the dilapidated governor's residence, denouncing the building as unsafe. The structure was a subject of an increasing number of negative editorials and articles in the press, to the great embarrassment of the legislature. Governor Brown was thus able to succeed in pushing for a new mansion. The legislature appropriated fifty thousand dollars to build a new residence for the state's governors. Completed in late 1871, it was heralded as a symbol of the bright future of the state of Missouri.

George Ingram Barnett, the architect chosen for the new mansion, was, in the nineteenth century, "Missouri's most distinguished architect,"[1] having designed many important Missouri homes before beginning work on the governor's mansion. The most notable of these preserved buildings are Selma Hall, also called Kennett Castle, thirty miles south of St. Louis, and the two Henry Shaw mansions in St. Louis. Born and trained in England, Barnett moved to the United States in 1839, and the talented young architect soon gained fame for his specialty, the Italian Renaissance style. He later formed an association with Albert Piquenard, who, while training in his native France, had become skilled in the French Renaissance style. The two styles influenced each other in the design of the Missouri governor's mansion. After 1860, the Second Empire style, with its Parisian roots, popularized mansard roofs and ironwork on balconies and rooflines. The Missouri mansion reflects this mixture of Italian Renaissance and French or Second Empire style. Some consider it one of the "finest examples of French-Italian architecture still standing in this country."[2]

The new mansion was built on the site of the old residence, high on the bluff overlooking the Missouri River. The three-story house's exterior is imbued with French and Italianate influences. Rose-colored brick trimmed in stone is topped with an exquisite sloping mansard roof and crowned with ornamental iron grillwork. The window sills, doors, and the corners of the building are framed in stone. The beautiful iron fence and stone wall that set two sides of the house off from the street predate the mansion.

The new residence was built in a little more than eight months at a final cost of seventy-five thousand dollars, which included the cost of some of the furnishings. In comparison to similar construction of the day, the time commitment was exceedingly short and the cost surprisingly low. According to Theodore Wofford, the lead architect of a team hired in the mid-1970s

1. Theodore J. Wofford, "The Missouri Executive Mansion: A Long Range Development Study," 5.
2. Marianna Riley, "Missouri's Mansion," *Missouri Life* 3, no. 6 (January–February 1976): 27.

to help guide the mansion's restoration, a like home in St. Louis built at the same time would have cost up to five hundred thousand dollars to build and would have taken two years to complete.[3] Because of financial constraints, however, there was an uneven quality in the building materials and, compared to similar buildings of the time, relatively sparse ornamentation in the finished building. For example, the pine moldings, windows, and door casements were painted, grained, and glazed to look like highly polished black walnut in order to match the central feature of the building—a real black walnut staircase.

There were no extra embellishments such as were typical of the day, and although only a minimal amount of ornamentation was used, it was carefully placed to maximize its effect. In this and similar ways, the architect, by being very selective, was able to overcome the funding limitations imposed on him and still design an elegant, durable structure spectacular in its simplicity and beautiful proportions. The building has lasted 131 years and is one of the oldest governors' mansions in the United States.

One outstanding feature of the home is the magnificent grand staircase, which has been called "one of the most beautiful free-flowing stairways in the country."[4] Seventeen-feet-high ceilings throughout the first and second floors contribute to the Classical style of the mansion's interior, creating a sense of orderly space and great openness for the house. The first floor contains the library, the great hall, the dining room, and the double parlor. Massive sliding doors open the rooms to the great hall and the parlors to each other.

The fifth occupant of the mansion, Governor Thomas T. Crittenden, served from 1879 to 1883 and was the first of many governors to spruce up the exterior by painting it red. With each new coat, the reds grew darker, until Mrs. Lloyd Stark, fifty years later, painted the entire exterior white, including the stone trim.

A tradition from the Gay Nineties has made it customary for official portraits of each governor's wife to be painted and hung in the mansion. When Governor and Mrs. Lon Stephens occupied the mansion at the turn of the century, their friends throughout the state contributed funds for her portrait, which began the tradition. The portraits of the state's first ladies are large oil paintings—colorful and complementary to the polished dignity of the interior of the mansion. Throughout the years, they have provided depth and warmth to the Missouri mansion and insight into the personalities of many of the women who have lived there. While many midwestern governors' mansions display pictures of first ladies, none of them are as large or as dramatic as the Missouri collection. Many of the Missouri portraits are the work of prominent Missouri artists such as Charles F. Galt, Fred Conway, and Gilbert Early.

Because of limited funds during the first third of the twentieth century, improvements to the mansion were minimal and largely cosmetic. As a result, the building deteriorated to such an extent that, in 1929, safety concerns caused Governor Henry S. Caulfield's inaugural recep-

3. Wofford, "The Missouri Executive Mansion: A Long Range Development Study."
4. *Past and Repast: The History and Hospitality of the Missouri Governor's Mansion*, 23.

tion to be moved to the capitol building. The mansion's greatest attraction, the grand staircase, which was designed to appear as if it has no visible support, was deemed unsafe for crowds.

When Governor and Mrs. Lloyd C. Stark moved into the house in 1937, the grand staircase was finally reinforced—steel brackets were used to prop and attach it to the wall. The landscaping was revitalized, and the Starks contributed thousands of new plants, including thirty- and forty-foot trees from their well-known Stark Nurseries located in Louisiana, Missouri.

After having served as governor in the 1940s, Governor Phil M. Donnelly was returned to the office in 1953. By this time, many Missouri legislators had become exasperated with the high cost of mansion maintenance. They thought the mansion ought to be demolished and replaced by a modern and more efficient governor's residence that would be less expensive to maintain. A bill was passed appropriating $250,000 for this purpose, but preservation-minded citizens were outspoken in their opposition to the legislature's plan of replacing a beautiful building full of heritage and history with a new one of no historical merit or significance. These citizens, recognizing the mansion as a landmark of great distinction, applauded Governor Donnelly's veto of the appropriation.

In 1958, the eloquent and persuasive Governor James T. Blair forced a major renovation appropriation for the mansion in a most compelling manner. Shortly after his inauguration, Governor Blair announced he would not bring his family to live in the governor's mansion, complaining that it had peeling wallpaper, worn-out plumbing, worm-eaten woodwork, and holes in the flooring of the first floor, and that it was infested with rats. Furthermore, he labeled the magnificent but sagging grand staircase "Cardiac Hill." Before taking office, Governor Blair suffered two heart attacks, which were not publicized. Doctors prohibited him from using the stairs. His bold statements were designed to force the installation of an elevator from the garage level to the second floor. The governor's pronouncements were widely publicized, and widespread recognition of the deterioration forced the Missouri legislature to appropriate funds for critical repairs, including the elimination of what was discovered to be thirty-eight rat nests, repairing the holes in the floor, repairing the plumbing and electrical systems, installing an elevator, and air-conditioning three rooms.

One of the most significant contributions to the restoration of the mansion was in returning the brickwork to its original state for the first time since 1881. When Warren G. Hearnes became governor in the middle of the 1960s, there were more than thirty-five coats of paint that needed to be removed from the house's exterior without damaging the brick. Mrs. Hearnes, recognizing the need for thoroughness yet extreme care, began the exterior restoration; under her supervision and that of state architect John D. Paulus Jr., a chemical wash was used to restore the exterior brick to its authentic appearance. The process took seven months—almost as long as it had taken to build the mansion in the first place. When the original rose-colored brick shone once more, it provided the perfect background for the pink granite pillars on the portico. These Corinthian columns were an original part of the mansion, gifts of Governor Gratz Brown, the stone having been mined from a granite quarry he owned near Ironton, Missouri.

Despite the fact that a large sum of money, about $390,000, was spent on refurbishing and repairing the mansion between 1957 and 1969, the building continued to decline and fade. There was no ongoing, long-term approach to planning for the upkeep of the mansion. It was a piecemeal process, and "renovation" had become an all-inclusive term used by first families in seeking appropriations from the legislature. As unforeseen problems occurred with the mansion, requests for emergency funding had to be approved. Performing the needed repairs and improvements in a crisis atmosphere resulted in inefficiencies accompanied by higher-than-necessary costs.

Governor Christopher "Kit" Bond, the twenty-eighth governor to reside in the mansion, took office in 1973. During each of his two nonconsecutive terms, Governor and Mrs. Bond provided leadership for a comprehensive restoration of the mansion. Mrs. Bond was instrumental in creating an ongoing group committed to taking care of the mansion. The organization, Missouri Mansion Preservation, Inc., or MMPI, was formed in October 1974 and enjoys the support of Missouri's former first ladies, many of the descendants of Missouri's first families, and other concerned individuals throughout the state.[5]

Carolyn Bond modeled the commission after the White House Fine Arts Committee. Clement Conger, the curator of that group, consulted with the Bonds about the formation and structure of MMPI. Mr. Conger attended the dedication of the mansion library in 1976.

With the creation of MMPI, arbitrary and whimsical alterations and additions to the mansion were no longer possible. Renovation decisions became subject to MMPI authorization. Some of the "aesthetic" contributions of former first ladies were removed or eliminated in order to restore the mansion to its original architectural harmony. The twenty-eight-member MMPI board is designed to be a nonpolitical panel of individuals who each have an interest in preserving the history of the mansion.

After MMPI authorized a study to determine and recommend the steps necessary to a complete restoration, a master plan was developed. Monies were raised from private and federal sources and the Missouri General Assembly for the step-by-step project. The work, led by Ted Wofford, a St. Louis restoration architect, was superbly and authentically executed in 1984. But there were also recommendations for replacement work that has not yet been required. For example, the slate mansard roof is not the same color or design as was the original. The plan is to make the correction when the time comes to replace the roof. Wofford's study has been a great public service because it details so much information about the mansion's origins, early years, and subsequent renovations. We now have a broad and deep knowledge of the house's structure, interior design, decor, and furnishings, intensifying our appreciation of its beauty.

Upon entering the Missouri governor's mansion, one first passes under the portico supported by the beautiful pink granite Corinthian columns and then through a pair of huge ornate front doors. They are hand carved, made from walnut, and weigh almost two thousand

5. Ibid., 47.

pounds each. Passing through the great hall into the double parlor and looking out enormous windows, one is treated to a view of the Missouri River that enhances the interior's dramatic sense of open space.

The interior of the mansion has been faithfully restored to the 1870s period in which it was built, staying true to the vision of the architect. The shades and hues of the walls, the wall coverings, the window coverings, and the floors and furniture are far from gloomy in their rich Victorian colors. All of the fluted columns and pilasters, whether separating the double parlors, setting off entrances, or framing the grand staircase, have been marbled, and the perimeters of the ceilings have been stenciled and gilded. The downstairs floors have been replaced; by the 1970s, the floors were no longer original to the house and were inconsistent with the quality and period of the house. The new floors, as suggested by Wofford, provide that consistency; they are a large-patterned parquet with borders of contrasting wood.

Early documentation showed that Renaissance Revival furniture had been purchased when the mansion was built in 1871; using this evidence, preservationists selected that style in order to integrate new acquisitions with existing pieces. The classical, large-scale Renaissance Revival furniture emphasizes carved and sculpted figures that make it highly decorative.

The dining-room sideboard is from the first Missouri governor's mansion, where it had been placed by Governor Edwards in 1844. A ten-piece parlor suite, one that once had been on display in the Smithsonian Institution's furniture exhibition "1876: A Centennial Exhibition," was purchased for the great hall. The fine antique furniture collection also includes gold-leaf chairs that were part of the Missouri exhibit at the St. Louis World's Fair in 1904; these are displayed in the ballroom on the third floor of the mansion.

Although the wives of many of Missouri's governors have been interested in mansion beautification, it was not until Carolyn Bond's vigorous pursuit of restoration and preservation that their intentions became a full reality. The Bonds sought to restore the early characteristics of the house so that, as renovation work became necessary in successive decades, any remedial changes would be within the dictates of historical accuracy. The accomplishments of previous first ladies, particularly Mrs. Stark, Mrs. Dalton, and Mrs. Hearnes, provided a setting to which Carolyn Bond brought her strong desire for heritage preservation, as well as her ability to raise large amounts of money—some two million dollars—from the private sector.

Mary Pat Abele, the executive director of MMPI, explains with pride the group's accomplishments: "Many experts consider the restoration of the Missouri Governor's Mansion to be the most authentic and carefully researched example of the Renaissance Revival period in the United States. It has been a privilege, as well as a rewarding experience, to coordinate the restoration of the Governor's Mansion and work with six first families in preserving this great Missouri landmark."[6] The changes to the house are documented in a book published in 1983, *Past and Repast,*

6. Mary Pat Abele, interview by author, Jefferson City, November 22, 2002.

a collaborative project led by Carolyn Bond with the MMPI. The book, as its name implies, chronicles the mansion's restoration while also serving as a hospitality book with menus.

Governor and Mrs. Mel Carnahan moved into the executive residence in 1992 and, like their predecessors, the Ashcrofts and the Bonds, continued the tradition of opening the mansion for public tours and events as well as using it as a site for public and private entertaining.

Jean Carnahan wrote books about the Missouri mansion while a resident there. The first, *If Walls Could Talk,* highlights the lives of the thirty families who have lived in the mansion. Another, *Christmas at the Mansion,* is a cookbook and memory book that describes the holiday celebrations of Missouri's first families, from early days to the present. As an advocate for the mansion, Mrs. Carnahan was an energetic and creative fund-raiser. In a 1997 letter reminding citizens that private funds provide for the upkeep of mansion furnishings, she included a color photograph of a Victorian chair that was losing its stuffing and in obvious need of new upholstery.

The grandeur of the Missouri governor's mansion is timeless—and with the care and interest taken in the mansion today, it is difficult to imagine that the old place could have once come so close to being given up for dead. The Missouri governor's mansion, designed more than a century ago by one of America's great architects, is not just architecturally significant, but one of the nation's foremost historic landmarks.

Evening view of front facade and fountain.

Ceiling detail.

The great hall featuring the Renaissance Revival
parlor suite that was exhibited in 1876.

Front view showing rose-colored brick, pink granite columns, mansard roof, and decorative ironwork.

Grand staircase with lady on the newel post.

Dining room, with portrait of Truman family.

View from the stairs, looking into great hall.

Double parlor, featuring some of the portraits of first ladies;
note the marbelized columns and decorative ceiling.

Library; note elaborate window treatments.

Nebraska
Governor's Mansion

Location: 1425 H Street, Lincoln

Construction Year: 1958

Cost: $259,000 (including furnishings)

Size: 15,000 square feet

Number of Rooms: 27

Architect: Selmer Solheim

Architectural Style: Modified Georgian Colonial

Furniture Style: A combination of Georgian,
   Empire, and Regency styles

Beginning with Lewis and Clark in 1804, and continuing for the next fifty years, explorers, trappers, missionaries, farmers, and gold seekers moved west, making trails through present-day Nebraska. Certainly by 1825—possibly as early as 1810—the American Fur Company established the first permanent settlement in Nebraska. As one historian summarized, "Nebraska's role was primarily that of providing a highway."[1]

Nebraska was organized as a territory in 1854, which officially opened it for white settlement, displacing and dispersing the Native American population. Throughout its territorial years, 1854–1867, everyday life in the Nebraska wilderness was harsh. The settlers used sod from the plains to construct houses that were not much more than shacks. The settlers, however, also began cultivating the land and planting crops, and these investments eventually paid enormous dividends. Nebraska's agricultural development became an economic mainstay of the country and permanently identified the state as one of the most important components of the nation's breadbasket.

When Nebraska joined the United States in 1867, there was a heated political competition for location of the new state's capital. There had been a similar contest during the territorial years, and for most of that time the capital had been Omaha. Almost immediately upon becoming a state, the legislature argued over a new site, and the capital site commissioners chose Lancaster, which was located in a saline region. They saw future potential for salt harvesting. Lancaster, with a population of about thirty, was renamed Lincoln; this new capital was only fifty-eight miles from Omaha. Construction of the state university in Lincoln and a railroad connection to the town gave investors more confidence in the future of the small village. By 1870, only three years after Nebraska achieved statehood, Lincoln's population had grown to twenty-five thousand. The plans for profiting through the development of the salt deposits did not materialize, however.

Nebraska's economy suffered in a financial panic that began in the East and spread across the country in the 1870s, profoundly affecting the agricultural marketplace. Nebraska farmers were unable to sell their corn and wheat at reasonable prices. Then, the Midwest suffered a major drought, as well as ongoing grasshopper plagues, both of which continued until late in the decade.

In this time of severe economic conditions, a bill to provide a governor's residence was introduced in the legislature, but it died from lack of attention. The concept of a dedicated governor's mansion was an idea whose time would not arrive for another twenty-six years. The economic problems, along with the sparse population of the state, fostered an egalitarian environment wherein the notion of providing a governor's residence probably seemed too elitist. Just as the territorial governors had done, the early state governors of Nebraska had to find their own housing, many of them living in boarding houses or hotels and some of them in their own homes.

1. James C. Olson, *History of Nebraska*, 42.

By the 1880s, Nebraska was becoming more prosperous. The droughts and the grasshoppers were gone, and with the improved agricultural environment, crop production more than tripled. By 1889, when Governor John M. Thayer held his inaugural reception in the state capitol building, the need for an official governor's residence was becoming obvious. And although an official residence was still years away, a thousand-dollar-a-year allocation was made to the governor for rent money.

By the late 1890s, Nebraska's pioneer years were over and its towns were becoming more urban. The governor's position at the top of the social structure began to force the legislature to view his needs as important. With this renewed interest in providing the governor with a place where he could both reside and entertain, in 1899 an appropriation of twenty-five thousand dollars was made to purchase Nebraska's first governor's residence.

The house chosen had recently been built by D. E. Thompson, a wealthy Lincoln businessman who later became the ambassador to Brazil. Thompson sold the state his two-and-a-half-story, white frame house for twenty-one thousand dollars. Although it was not overly ornate, it was considered a beautiful house. In newspapers and other publications the design of the house is sometimes described as Queen Anne Colonial style and sometimes as Neoclassical Revival style. The house had elements of both styles and was not a pure version of either. Many late Victorian-era homes were a combination of the Queen Anne and the Classical Revival styles.

The Queen Anne style of architecture is based on romanticism. It is called "picturesque" because it displays combinations of decorative materials, such as shingles and trims, that create a colorful, vivid, and ornamental look. The style is irregular and allows for variety in the floor plan and imagination in the details. There are turrets, porticoes, and multipaned, multicolored windows. One architectural historian described other elements this way: "Queen Anne chimneys are tall, [and] choke-topped. . . . Most Queen Anne supporting columns on porches and porte-cocheres have an upside-down look. They are wide at the top and flared out with decorative brackets."[2]

In America, the Queen Anne style of the 1870s and 1880s gave way to Classicism toward the end of the century. Many of the transitional houses of the day borrowed from both styles. For example, the Nebraska governor's mansion, while it had a wrap-around porch in the Queen Anne style, also had dentil molding under the eaves of the house—a Classical Revival element that was becoming popular. The exterior of the house was balanced, well-ordered, and symmetrical; it did not contain a lot of variation or irregularity. And its columns were Doric rather than the previously mentioned "upside-down" ones that were seen in many pure Queen Anne–style homes. But some of the interior elements were more typically Queen Anne, such as the dining-room alcove, the oak spindles and the fretwork in the foyer—all elements of that style.

The Thompson mansion served as a home for Nebraska governors for fifty-seven years, but

2. Harry Devlin, *Portraits of American Architecture: A Gallery of Victorian Homes,* 132.

by 1945 the house had become old and drafty and had outlived its usefulness. Its antiquated electrical and plumbing systems needed to be replaced, and the feasibility of continued investment in this old house was under constant review. Additionally, the social entertainment requirements of the governors had become more complex, and the house was too small to fill those needs while at the same time affording a comfortable family life for its residents. Thus, in 1945 the legislature appropriated a hundred thousand dollars to build a new official residence. Implementation of the legislature's action was delayed, and in 1955 the original appropriation was increased to two hundred thousand. A provision was incorporated into the legislation that the money had to be used to build a new mansion and not to renovate an old structure.

Nebraska's decision against renovation probably had two sources. First, there was the ongoing difficulty and expense the state had been encountering for so long in keeping the old house in shape. Second, throughout postwar America, there was a general postwar attitude that new things were better than things with age: "The favorite solution was to start afresh. Old buildings were demolished to give way to new."[3] The need to preserve older homes was too much of a minority viewpoint to enable restoration of the original Nebraska governor's mansion.

Thus the old house was demolished, and the use of the same property for the new mansion provided the only continuity between old and new. The two mansions—the current one and the one that exists now only in memory—occupy almost exactly the same site; this location is the legacy of the original house that lives on with the new.

Nebraska's towering state capitol building stands directly across the street from the governor's residence. It soars four hundred feet heavenward, while the residence, in contrast, is a long, horizontal, two-story building. The capitol is constructed of limestone and marble augmented with beautiful American and European elements and has been nationally acclaimed by architects. It was built some twenty years before the governor's mansion, and it is generally considered to be the most significant piece of architecture in Nebraska.

For the governor's residence, Selmer Solheim, a local architect, designed what he called a modified Georgian Colonial house. Many houses built in the fifties adopted historical motifs or explored a "pseudohistorical styling of the past."[4] The Colonial style was so popular that it was incorporated into new construction at every price level.

Significant controversy surrounded the design of the Nebraska mansion. Although the State Building Commission made the final decision, choosing from seven submitted designs, it did so in concert with the architect and with Governor and Mrs. Victor E. Anderson.

Constructed in 1958, the fifteen-thousand-square-foot mansion cost $259,000 to construct and furnish. The Colonial style fueled a controversy that was characterized in the press as a "war of taste." Supporters of the Colonial house considered the design to be tried and true, while dissenters considered it to be a stereotypical, copycat design that had no meaning for Nebraska. Newspaper articles from the era reveal that the design was selected because it was

3. Witold Rybczynski, *City Life: Urban Expectations in a New World*, 160.
4. Ralph W. Hammett, *Architecture in the United States: A Survey of Architectural Styles since 1776*, 288.

traditional—it was neither modern nor contemporary—and the architect and the governor were pleased with the choice. As Solheim, the architect, explained in the *Lincoln Journal,* August 20, 1956: "[A] style which leaned heavily on our basic American heritage might more soundly approach the permanency desired in the style of a building for a governor's mansion. . . . [C]ontemporary styles might appear quite dated 25–35 years from now."

Despite the controversy, the finished product is a solidly built house with all sorts of modern conveniences and amenities. Moreover, in terms of size, comfort, and efficiency, it has answered the needs of the governors who have resided there and it is genuinely described as dignified, gracious, and restrained.

Nebraska's mansion is built of smooth pink double-sized brick and has white Colonial pillars and trim. It sits back from the street, giving it a large sweep of a front yard. The front approach is by way of a double-lane circular drive; the orderly landscape enhances the house's well-proportioned appearance.

Visitors enter through an attractive vestibule with a slate floor and proceed into a large, white-marble foyer with a dramatic and unusual elliptical staircase trimmed in white-painted wrought iron.

The living room of the house is generally referred to as the "state drawing room." It is large enough to accommodate official receptions; by employing different seating arrangements, the governor can host both large and small groups. A hand-carved white pine mantelpiece surrounds the oversized fireplace, which is a focal point in the room. Another focal point in this large room is a colorful symbolic painting that was commissioned in 1998, *Capitol Seasons,* by Allan Tubach, one of Nebraska's best-known painters. The painting hangs over the sofa and features the capitol tower, the Platte River, and parts of historic houses, churches, and elements of university buildings, all in Lincoln. The Platte River symbolizes Lincoln's ties with the other parts of Nebraska. A third focal point in the state drawing room is an Empire sofa, which was original to the old house and belonged to that mansion's first owner, D. E. Thompson.

The drawing room is otherwise furnished predominantly in the Regency and the Empire periods. Some of the important features of the new mansion, like the Empire sofa, were rescued from the old mansion and therefore serve as a link to the past. The oak paneling and marble fireplace in the governor's library are also from the old governor's residence. The paneling in the foyer of the old mansion made a strong statement about the quality of the old house, and it was a good plan to bring it into the new. These features add an old-fashioned shine to the state drawing room and the library.

The public rooms of the Nebraska mansion are on the first floor and the lower level; the first family's living quarters are on the second floor. The lower level contains meeting space large enough for oversized groups. Large sit-down luncheons and dinners that cannot be accommodated in the dining room are held here. This lovely room has remarkable lighting and comfortable decor that includes a fireplace.

One of the most colorful of the public rooms is the first-floor dining room, whose furnishings are Williamsburg and Georgian reproductions. The room's classical features include crown molding with dentil detail, and Georgian pilasters with a pediment, which frame the serving buffet. An impressive array of silver is displayed in this room. However, it is the outstanding Zuber scenic wood-block wallpaper that provides the room's color. Designed in France in 1834, it contains 223 different colors. Chosen and installed during the 1998 renovation, it is the twin to wallpaper in the White House. The paper is entitled "Scenic America" and depicts a sequence of scenes of American landscapes, cities, and people organized around five vignettes of old historic American places.

Looking out the dining room's large bay window to the backyard, one sees a fountain and a stream created with natural materials; native plants line the banks. The landscaping plan defines this large property by separating the extensive patio areas and their gardens and by grading them to make different levels.

In 1987 Nebraska elected a female governor, Kay Orr. During her term, her husband wrote *The First Gentleman's Cookbook* as a fund-raiser for the residence. The book earned sixty thousand dollars, which, along with other contributions, was placed in an endowment that today continues to generate interest income to benefit the mansion. Bill Orr later became one of the chairmen in the fund-raising campaign for the 1998 renovation.

Governor E. Benjamin Nelson became the tenth governor to occupy the governor's residence. Shortly after his 1990 election, Governor and Mrs. Nelson announced a $1 million statewide fund-raising drive to renovate the governor's mansion. But when the actual renovation was launched in 1997, the goal was increased to $4 million. This brought the decades-old design conflict back to the surface; an example of some of the public's misgivings appeared in a letter, published on March 26, 1997, that Nebraskan Michael C. Stuart wrote to the *Lincoln Journal Star:* "If we are going to spend $4 million . . . let's tear down the existing colonial monstrosity and build a mansion that is just as awesome and compliments the art deco style of the Capitol building."

Despite such criticism, Governor and Mrs. Nelson's campaign to raise renovation money was a huge success. Almost $2.5 million was raised from private sources alone. The changes that came with the improvements amounted to a complete renewal for the governor's residence, quelling the earlier controversy.

The vernacular architecture of the state capitol echoes the western plains and reflects the prosperity of Nebraska's cattle and farming businesses. The dome, for example, honors the state's agricultural roots, with a bronze statue of a man sowing grain at the top. The entire capitol is imbued with meaningful images, including interior mosaic murals and exterior sculptures, all symbolic of the state, that honor Nebraska's heritage. The famous building, designed by Bertram G. Goodhue, is a wonderful illustration of Nebraska history.

The governor's mansion, however, was not built as a monument or a museum. It has fulfilled the expectations of its planners and builders by being a solid, enduring, and useful structure reflecting permanency, stability, and formality. While Lincoln, Nebraska, has countless buildings of important architectural design and history, the governor's residence was never intended to serve as a historical marker. In its official capacity as a home for the governors, it plays a number of important roles. It not only houses the governor, providing the governor's family with privacy and dignified quarters while also providing a place for the governor to officially entertain, but it also promotes goodwill in the community through the use of its meeting spaces for community meetings. And like other governors' mansions, it extends hospitality to visiting dignitaries. Nebraska's governor's mansion provides for the needs of its chief executive; considering that, it is arguably the most important house in the state.

Foyer featuring wrought-iron staircase.

Living-room view from foyer, showing the antique sofa with
symbolic painting that was commissioned for the mansion.

Front of Nebraska governor's mansion.

Rear exterior of house and fountain
with capitol in the background.

North Dakota
Governor's Mansion

Location: 1311 North 14th Street, Bismarck

Construction Year: 1960

Cost: $170,000

Size: 10,000 square feet

Number of Rooms: 18

Architect: Ritterbush Brothers

Architectural Style: Ranch

Furniture Style: Transitional

North Dakota is not merely a state: It is a larger-than-life frontier setting and a place where one's imagination can capture almost every colorful western notion. Occupying an enormous terrain with a great deal of empty space and with no large urban area, the state serves as a screening room for playing back our basic assumptions, part reality and part myth, about Western history and culture.

When we say "North Dakota," our minds conjure up wind and dust on the open expanses of the badlands; Teddy Roosevelt hunting buffalo, antelope, and deer; Indians in elaborate dress dancing at a powwow; cowboys on horseback, brandishing pistols for practice and long arms for killing game; and the settlers and homesteaders trudging through the ache and crunch of frozen snow to the crude warmth of their sod or tar-paper shacks.

While the North and South were preparing for Civil War, many westering settlers were preoccupied with obtaining land from Indians and creating the Dakota Territory. As the war began in 1861, the Dakota Territory was just emerging. It included what we know today as North Dakota, South Dakota, Montana, and parts of Idaho and Wyoming, with the territorial capital being located in Yankton, at the confluence of the Missouri and James Rivers, at the southern end of the vast territory.

The inhabitants of the Dakota Territory were not interested in imitations of eastern culture, nor were they motivated by a desire for a refined social structure. The territory was a place where hard work was the dominating characteristic of the settler; it was a place where people had few illusions, a gigantic and empty place susceptible to the harshest of winter weather.

And things have not changed that much. On December 19, 1996, an article in the *St. Louis Post-Dispatch* describing a recent blizzard quoted Dan Stewart, a North Dakota farmer: "This is when survival and protecting what feeds you and your family is most important, and what you look like and all those glamorous things are the last thing on your mind. It gets down to where it's simply survival."

In 1883 the territorial capital was moved from Yankton to Bismarck, igniting a building boom there. The city was located at a crossing point of the Missouri River, along the railroad serving the territory, and close to the geographical center of the territory. Bismarck became caught up in the spirit of expansion, and a wave of new construction was launched; within a month after its selection as the capital, a new penitentiary, a state capitol building, and over 160 houses were under construction.

The new affluence also meant that a few entrepreneurs were becoming rich and able to build luxurious two- and three-story frame houses. One of these businessmen was Asa Fisher, an early settler who in 1872 started selling supplies from a tent on the banks of the Missouri River. A year later he moved his merchandising operation two miles back from the river to the newly named town of Bismarck, where he added a liquor business. As his business prospered, he became an organizer and the president of the First National Bank of Bismarck and the owner of a considerable amount of real estate.

In 1884, Fisher built a house that was "large, comfortable and elegant, with black walnut trimmings and casings which are the finest and the most costly in the city."[1] It was a two-and-a-half-story, multigabled, two-toned green Victorian mansion with solid walnut and cherry woodwork. The house stood alone, at the edge of town, on the corner of a dirt road. The showy sides of the property were fenced with iron that matched the cresting on the roof of the house; the less notable sides were fenced in plain wood.

Asa Fisher's house was built in the late Victorian period and is an example of the Stick style of architecture, a style of wooden domestic architecture. The Stick style of wooden building was oriented to the country and was influenced by democratic and utilitarian ideals. Popular for its simplicity, it represented a break from the complex, grand previous styles. Fisher's house incorporates some decorative elements of the Queen Anne style, which was also popular in the Victorian era.

In 1889 the Dakota Territory was divided into North and South Dakota, and the two new states entered the Union. Although there was no U.S. law prohibiting alcohol until 1918, the residents of the newly formed North Dakota included an article establishing prohibition in their first state constitution. This made Asa Fisher's liquor trade illegal and forced him to close his business. He sold his home to the state in 1893 and moved to Colorado, where he opened another wholesale liquor business.

North Dakota was by no means a wealthy state, but from the beginning of statehood the legislature recognized the importance of providing a place for the governor to reside. Although the Fisher House was one of the fanciest houses in Bismarck, it was not chosen to be the governor's residence because it was considered a mansion, but rather because it was available, comfortable, and stylish, reminiscent of frontier days and yet easily adaptable for the needs of a governor. Thus North Dakota provided its governor with a residence only four years after statehood—a shorter period than with any other state in the Midwest. Funds were appropriated by the North Dakota legislature in 1893, and the Fisher House was purchased for a little over five thousand dollars. It was occupied by governors and their families from 1893 until 1960. The first to reside in the new residence was Governor Eli C. D. Shortridge.

Initially, there were no protective restraints preventing the occupants of the historic house from making changes to the residence. Consequently, in the early years, between 1907 and 1919, the governor's mansion underwent its greatest departure from its intended original appearance. Governor John Burke made the most obvious visible change by screening in the verandas and painting the house white, thereby removing much of the traditional Victorian color. Next, Governor Louis Hanna took down the original iron fence surrounding the house, which made the property appear less distinctive. Then, Governor Lynn J. Frazier ruined the Victorian appearance of the house by removing the original front porches and the associated

1. *Bismarck Tribune,* October 3, 1884, quoted in Virginia L. Heidenreich, *North Dakota's Former Governors' Mansion: Its History and Presentation,* 4.

decorative trim that skirted the house, and replacing them with a two-story, full-front screened porch. In subsequent years, random interior changes occurred when one or another governor would remove a fireplace, a mantlepiece, the fretwork separating the two front parlors, and even an original mirror. Since there was no plan that mandated systematic maintenance of the original appearance, modifications in response to stated needs or prevailing trends and gubernatorial whims were unrestricted.

As early as 1929, the state began to give serious consideration to acquiring a new governor's mansion. A fund was established at that time, but its availability expired before it could be put to use. Because of other pressing needs, it was not until 1955, during the third term of Governor C. Norman Brunsdale, that the state was able to enact a bill calling for a new residence. The legislation authorized two hundred thousand dollars for the design and construction of a new house for the state's chief executive.

The architectural firm of Leonhard and Askew was hired to design the new governor's residence. The specifications required that the building contain enough space for the family living quarters as well as for meeting space and official entertaining. The Bismarck architects submitted plans for a modern, wood, brick, and glass structure that the state's board of administration considered impractical and too expensive. The architectural firm was discharged and paid seven thousand dollars for its time and trouble.

Eventually, in the summer of 1958, another Bismarck firm, Ritterbush Brothers, was hired to design the new mansion. This design was accepted, and the new residence was completed in March 1960.

For a short time the old executive mansion was used for the offices of the State Health Department. In 1959, however, Arthur A. Link, a member of the North Dakota House of Representatives, had the wisdom and foresight to present a bill to the legislature calling for the restoration of the old mansion as a state historic site. Approval was granted in the 1959 legislative session.

Link became governor in 1973 and through his leadership the Society for the Preservation of the Former Governor's Mansion was organized to keep the house from deteriorating and to promote its preservation. Since 1975 the State Historical Society of North Dakota has been responsible for the maintenance of the old mansion, and in that year the building was entered in the National Register of Historic Places. This is one of fifty-six historic sites under the State Historical Society's management.

Researched, restored, and over a hundred years old, by 1985, the old brewer's house, with its original white oak staircase, which was described as "the best house in the state," was polished up and made into the newest museum in North Dakota.[2] The exterior of the house was restored to its appearance at the time it was purchased by the state—1893. In order to demonstrate how the house was used during the occupancies of the twenty-one governors who had

2. *Bismarck Tribune,* May 24, 1985.

called it home, interior restoration exhibits show the wallpapers, paint colors, furnishings, and architectural details from the different eras. The exhibits and the restoration serve to reassure the public that although the beautiful house's colors might begin to fade, it won't be for long. The house has been and will continue to be renewed with historical accuracy. North Dakotans call their revered, restored, older residence the "governor's mansion," and the new house the "governor's residence."

The current residence was built for $170,000, which left about $30,000 of the 1955 appropriation for furnishings. The new mansion is located on the capitol grounds a few blocks from the old mansion. The state capitol mall and nearby area is a historic district of 140 acres containing landmark chunks of North Dakota history. At its entrance is a statue of a pioneer family, and throughout the park are historical markers reflecting the state's history. In addition to statues of a buffalo and a horse, there is an arresting bronze statue honoring Sakakawea. She was the young Shoshone woman who became famous for the importance of her role as interpreter in the Lewis and Clark expedition in 1804. This original monument, Sakakawea with her baby on her back, has been on the capitol grounds since 1910. A replica of it stands in the U.S. Capitol in Washington, D.C., representing North Dakota in Statuary Hall.

The new residence is a rambling, L-shaped, split-level ranch house inspired by the designs of Frank Lloyd Wright and built from redwood and North Dakota rough-wire brick that was manufactured in Hebron, North Dakota; the clay for this type of brick is shaped by moving a wire through it, which gives it a rough texture. The house sits on an angle in order for the living room and dining room to have a view of the capitol. The floor plan has over ten thousand square feet of space, including offices for the governor and his wife, private family quarters, and, on the lower level, a very large multipurpose room that can be used as space for staff meetings or private family space, as determined by the incumbent first family.

Minnesota granite lines the walls of the main foyer and the fireplace. The original floor of the foyer was New England slate before a 1999 renovation changed the floor to marble and painted the granite walls a lighter sandstone color. In 1992, the original kitchen was completely replaced, and the governor's office space was reconfigured to give both the kitchen and the office a view of the backyard and the capitol.

In 1986, the Friends of the North Dakota Governor's Residence, a nonpartisan, not-for-profit fund-raising organization, was formed to raise private funds necessary to supplement legislative appropriations for the house. There is also a Capital Arts and Historic Preservation Committee that acts as an advisory commission; its approval is required before significant changes or renovations can be made to the governor's residence. The two groups have separate but important functions: one raises money, and the other plans and coordinates changes to the building.

Some of the furniture is original to the house, but most, along with the carpets and draperies, has been replaced. The original modern furniture was subdued, made of warm-looking natural woods, and was not the kind of "contemporary" style that was shiny, bold, or intrusive—but it had a hard life. The volume of visitors to the residence takes its toll. The house is graciously opened for community events and meetings. The new furniture chosen to replace the original is sturdy, solid, and built to last. It is best described as transitional in style; it blurs the line between the original modern and a more traditional or classical style.

The governor's residence is quiet, gracious, and gives no sense of pretense or grandiosity. It is immaculately maintained and sits on an oversized, well-manicured lawn, planted to perfection with shrubs, trees, and flowers. The house faces a neighborhood street of plain houses that are not in any way fancy. Setting it apart geographically from the neighborhood are a huge display of elm trees—American elm (the official state tree), Siberian elm, and Chinese elm. The cedar rail backyard fence was inspired by the Secret Service's action in 1989 when it canceled President George Bush's horseshoe match against Governor George Sinner for lack of a fenced border protecting the president. Now the fence and its landscaping look as if they have always been there. Ponderosa pines wrap around the outside of the fence, and lilacs bank the inside.

There is a simple open freshness to the North Dakota residence—pared down and unencumbered by superfluous space. There is a noticeable absence of servants' quarters. And yet, the organization and smooth operation of the house demonstrate the efficiency of expert management. The residence has a vitality—a livable and unpretentious style—all its own.

Wood is an architectural feature that visually links North Dakota's governors' mansions to each other. The mansions were built almost a hundred years apart, and yet they are compatible with their environment, and both fit perfectly into their setting. The different styles of the houses represent the decades in which they were built, but each style stays true to a rugged western or northern spirit through its use of natural materials.

One could easily view the current governor's residence of North Dakota as a metaphor for the state. Like the state, the mansion is uncrowded, serene, and friendly. It is redolent of the durable traditions and fortitude of a state that has been forged from the harshness of its historical past. The materials used in the house—wood, granite, slate, marble, and brick—are as sturdy and substantial as the natural elements of the frontier and the strong spirit of its citizens. As North Dakota progresses into the twenty-first century, one has the feeling that this is one governor's mansion that will endure, never needing to be drastically altered or rearranged, or that, if someday it has to be replaced, it will be by a building designed to endure and to enhance the image of North Dakota in the manner of the present residence.

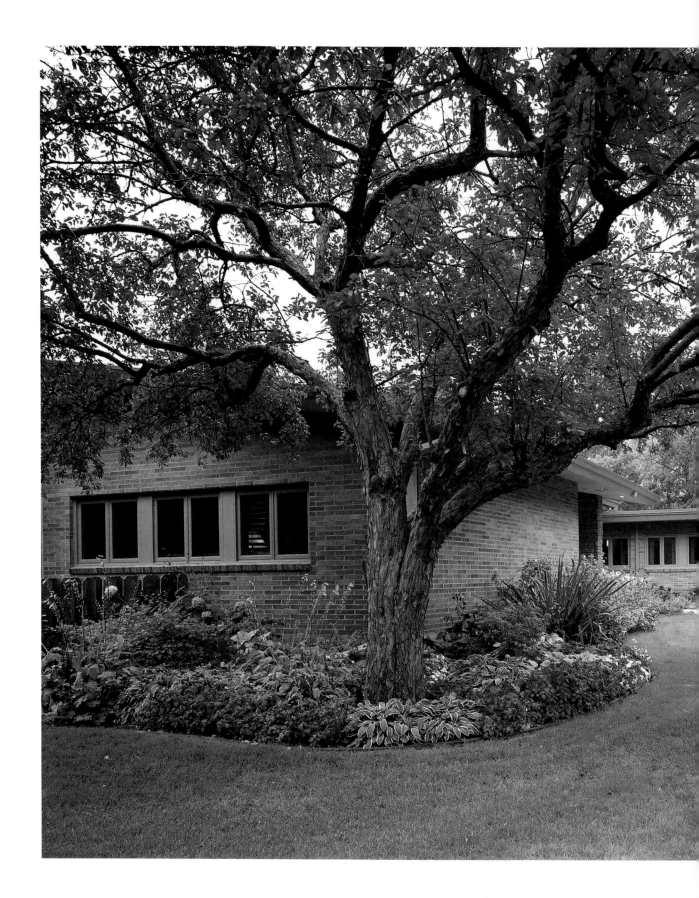

Angled front facade of the
present governor's residence.

Dining room view, from the living room.

Living room, from the foyer.

The historic original governor's
mansion, built in 1884.

Ohio
Governor's Mansion

National Register of Historic Places

Location: 358 North Parkview Drive, Columbus

Construction Year: 1925

Cost: $35,000

Size: 8,400 square feet

Number of Rooms: 25

Architect: Robert Gilmore Hanford

Architectural Style: Jacobean Revival

Furniture Style: Mixed-English antiques
   and reproductions

If Arthur St. Clair had had his way, the state of Ohio would still be part of the Northwest Territory. Territorial Governor St. Clair battled the notion of Ohio's becoming a state. He cited everything—from the distance between the federal government and the outpost, to his assessment that the settlers were too few, too dumb, and too uninformed to be trusted with votes. But in the end his obstinacy was his undoing. To protect federalism and his own position, St. Clair had used methods that were autocratic and dictatorial, violating the premises of democracy. President Thomas Jefferson removed him from office in 1802 and then appointed Edward Tiffin as the first governor of the new state of Ohio in 1803.

In Ohio's early years, the capital moved from Chillicothe to Zanesville and back to Chillicothe. In 1812, state lawmakers finally settled on a patch of wilderness close to the middle of the state and situated on the banks of the Scioto and Olentangy Rivers; this would become the future state capital. They named the site for Christopher Columbus and soon started building from scratch this future capital city of Ohio.

Thomas Worthington, brother-in-law of Governor Edward Tiffin, became the sixth governor (1814–1818). During his tenure, the capital was officially moved to Columbus, where it remains today. But in 1812, before the capital move, and in its first year, the population of Columbus went from zero to three hundred.

Dr. John Cotton, a physician from Massachusetts who settled in Ohio, described Columbus in its third year: "The streets are filled with stumps of trees and environed with woods, which give the town the appearance of having just emerged from the forest. . . . The people have been collected from every quarter and having great diversity of habits and manners, of course, do not make the most agreeable company."[1] He mentioned with some surprise that Columbus had grown to seven hundred people and two hundred houses in its first three years. His observation about the inhabitants of early Columbus can be attributed to the diversity in Ohio's settlement patterns. Northeastern Ohio was settled by New Englanders, largely from Connecticut and Massachusetts, while the southern part of the state was settled by Virginians; in the middle were settlers from the Middle Atlantic states.

Ohio legislators took their time in making a decision about providing an official residence for their governors. While discussions and arguments, for and against, droned on in the legislature, forty-eight successive governors lived in taverns or hotels, in rented rooms, or in their own houses. Then, well over a century later, the legislature finally reached a decision, and the first official governor's mansion became a reality in 1919.

Although Ohio did not own a governor's mansion during the Civil War, one elegant house became an unofficial governor's residence. Counting it, the first official governor's mansion, and the mansion that is in use today, Ohio has had three important houses used as governors' mansions since 1862. All of these are still standing. They are historical and classical, but none are grandiose. Each of Ohio's residences has provided an important, gracious setting for the governor and his family without communicating a feeling of pretension or royalty.

1. Quoted in Rufus King, *Ohio: First Fruits of the Ordinance of 1787,* 340.

The very first residence was owned privately and was loaned to Governor David Tod in the early years of the Civil War. Built in 1852 by Philip T. Snowden, a successful merchant, it is considered the finest example of Italianate architecture in Columbus. Its red-brick exterior is soft and warm and set off by ornate and carefully embellished, tall, arched windows. The building was later damaged by fire and rebuilt in 1872 by the prominent local architect George Bellows Sr., father of George Bellows, the famous artist who lived in Ohio and New York in the early 1900s. No one is certain who the building's original architect was, but George Bellows Sr. had moved to Columbus in 1849, and it is quite possible that he designed the house, although the information was never recorded. Kylie Towers, archivist and curator for the Heritage Museum, an educational outreach project of the Kappa Kappa Gamma Foundation, has researched the pertinent records and found no listing for the original architect of the building. Today that historic building, which ceased to be used as a governor's mansion in 1864, is both the Heritage Museum and the national headquarters of Kappa Kappa Gamma Fraternity; it has been included on the National Register of Historic Places.

In 1917, the Ohio legislature had appropriated $125,000 to purchase a lot and construct a residence, but almost immediately the legislature decided instead that it would be better to purchase an existing house.

The Charles H. Lindenberg home was a thirty-room mansion with a third-floor ballroom, built in 1904 in the Georgian Revival Eclectic style of architecture. The Eclectic period was epitomized by mixed architectural styles. The Lindenberg House was purchased for seventy-five thousand dollars and then renovated; in 1920, it was first occupied by Governor and Mrs. James A. Cox. Ten first families called this mansion home until it was converted in 1957 to house Ohio's state archives; today it is the office of the Ohio Foundation. The 1957 conversion was not controversial; at that point, the house needed expensive renovation—and the timing turned out to almost coincide with a gift to the state of a new residence.

This residence was a twenty-five-room house that had been built in 1925 for the manufacturer Malcolm Jeffrey. Malcolm's father, Joseph Jeffrey, the founder of Jeffrey Manufacturing Company, had built the house for his son. Malcolm and his family lived there until his death in 1936, at which time the home was sold to his sister, Florence Jeffrey Carlile. She lived there until her death in 1955, when the house passed on to her daughter, Janet Harris. Janet, who was married to the Episcopal bishop of Chicago, had no need for the Ohio home. Recognizing that it would make a fine residence for the governors of Ohio, Bishop and Mrs. Harris generously offered it to the state and, in 1955, the legislature authorized Governor Frank Lausche to accept the gift. In 1957, Governor and Mrs. William O'Neil were the first gubernatorial family to occupy the new mansion. But none of the first families who lived there, including the O'Neils, did anything to promote the original intention of how the house should look, until Governor Celeste took office in 1983.

This house, like the Lindenberg House, is located in suburban Bexley, four miles from Ohio's state capitol building. Between 1870 and the 1920s, Bexley transformed from a rural area where cows grazed, and where citizens occupied a few small homes and farms, to an exclusive urban retreat, where Columbus's leading businessmen and industrialists lived in large homes with beautiful parks. The stately homes and large lot sizes were all the rage in the 1920s when wealthy individuals surrounded their residences with spacious grounds reminiscent of English country estates. The name Bexley was taken from surveying books from the County of Kent in England.

The Jeffrey House was designed by a local Columbus architect, Robert Gilmore Hanford. He built many of the houses in Bexley. The house style is usually referred to as Jacobean Revival, but in some sources it is occasionally referred to as Tudor Norman. Although both designations are accurate, the brochures published by the governor's mansion designate it Jacobean. The house is a combination of styles, and one sees Tudor as well as French influences. The Jacobean type generally is a Tudor-style house, usually built between 1900 and 1930. Hanford created a house that looks like a grand manor, and its emphasis on gables, bay windows, and timbered ceilings show the English castle influence. Houses built in this manner were loosely based on sixteenth- and seventeenth-century English models using many different building materials, as did the English, and freely using several building methods. For example, in the Jeffrey House, one finds rough stone as well as stuccoed walls. There is an oriel window (a bay window located above the first-floor level) that has stone mullions, but there is also a two-story bay window with timbered mullions. This stately building of Ohio limestone, brick, stucco, and wood, with its leaded-glass windows and slate roof, looks like an imposing, first-rate English manor house.

Governor James A. Rhodes served four terms but lived in the governor's mansion only during his first two terms, from 1963 to 1971. The building had deteriorated, and during his next two terms, from 1975 until 1983, Governor and Mrs. Rhodes lived in their private home. An article about the livability of the mansion during the Rhodes administration in the *Akron-Beacon Journal* of March 18, 1984, reported, "Ceilings and walls were cracked and peeling; the kitchen was a shambles; it needed a new roof, new windows and new wiring."

Since Governor Rhodes had left the building vacant for eight years, minimal maintenance had been done when its next occupants, Governor and Mrs. Richard F. Celeste, moved into the mansion. The house was a mess and needed a complete overhaul. The wiring and the windows had to be replaced and the roof and pipes redone, but after plastering, painting, sanding, and polishing, the house began to return to its former beauty. Governor and Mrs. Celeste understood the importance of recreating the house's original atmosphere as a grand manor house. In all the time the state had owned the house, such renovation had not been attempted—only updating and decorating in piecemeal attempts by the various first families. Eventually the true nature of the house would have become obliterated.

Governor Celeste established the Friends of the Residence, a private group charged with raising money for restoration and refurbishing. Also at this time, the house's official designation was changed from governor's mansion to governor's residence. Additionally, it was during the Celeste administration that the governor's residence was included on the National Register of Historic Places.

Governor George V. Voinovich was inaugurated in 1991 and served two terms. In 1995, he established the Governor's Residence Advisory Commission. This panel oversees the historic preservation and restoration of the home. It is also the authority that determines and oversees capital improvements and articulates the need for preserving and protecting the continuity and future of the residence. There is also a Governor's Residence Foundation that helps raise and contribute money for mansion projects. Mrs. Voinovich was personally active in mansion-preservation issues.

The Voinoviches lived in the residence and cared for it as if it were a slowly aging, beloved family member, and today the house conveys a powerful legacy, glowing with the attention and care it receives. Governor and Mrs. Robert A. Taft continue the practice of responsible stewardship. They maintain and preserve the house and its furnishings with great respect; at the same time, they are also collecting information about the governor's residence in order to establish an archive to be kept in the home. Governor Taft is the great-grandson of President William Howard Taft, twenty-seventh president of the United States.

Since Governor Celeste's administration, massive renovations and comprehensive maintenance plans have truly made a difference to the Ohio governor's residence. Brand-new life was pumped into the twenty-five-room jewel, bringing it back to respectability.

The impressive estate sits on a three-and-a-half acre lot under a canopy of vintage trees. The magnificent grounds include a wide, curved drive that does not detract from the property; rather, it emphasizes the graceful landscaping and classical outdoor design.

The heavy wooden front door is recessed in a limestone arched entry. This is typical of a Tudor or a Jacobean Revival house. Stepping into the large entrance hall, one immediately notices the tone of cool serenity in this formal yet welcoming place. Its hand-hewn ceiling beams and native limestone walls are further testament to the warm feelings and cool countenance offered by old stone buildings shaded by old trees. In addition, the oak beams provide weighty counterpoint to the white plaster ceiling's molded design.

To the left of the entrance hall is a walnut-paneled dining room, and to the right is a large step-down living room. An elegant walnut grand staircase leads to the second and third floors, where the governor's family have their private living quarters. Originally the second and third floors each contained nine bedrooms.

The living room has oak-paneled walls, a patterned plaster ceiling, and a tremendous fireplace. Leaded-glass doors flanking the fireplace open to the study, and other leaded-glass doors lead to the stone-walled garden room. In addition to the first-floor public rooms used for living and entertaining, there is a service wing that houses the kitchen and pantry.

The interior furnishings, both antique and reproduction pieces, complement the Jacobean style of architecture. There is an intentional mixture of periods and styles; the resulting effect reminds one of an English country house with furniture that has been collected for generations, making a casual but caring statement. The dining-room furniture, as well as a cupboard and a desk, are original to the house. Some of the living-room furniture was made for the house in 1992; it is large in scale and Jacobean in style. Mrs. Voinovich sent a small branch from one of the buckeye trees on the residence's grounds to a skilled wood craftsman for him to use as a model in carving a fine collection of furniture. This furniture maker, Brandon Thomas, copied the buckeye motif and created a beautiful settee, four stools, and eight chairs. Using Honduran mahogany, Thomas made pieces that stand out as formal reminders of the buckeye, the Ohio state tree. They are used in different rooms on the first floor. Other pieces have been gathered from various sources, including the home's original owners, the Jeffrey and Carlile families.

The garden room serves as a natural connection to the outside gardens and walkway. A vine-covered pergola leads from just outside the garden room to the lawn and garden. Inside and outside, the house is in complete harmony, and as one would expect, the landscaping is also meticulously planned. The limestone patios and walkway contribute to the enduring look of the house's architecture.

As an example of the Tudor Norman or Jacobean style, this massive house exhibits the European roots that dominated architectural themes in the early twentieth century. Meanwhile, its powerful presence is not intimidating or overpowering. Nothing about its understated demeanor suggests that it should be a museum.

From its multiple chimneys and detailed chimney pots to its six fireplaces and fine French doors, this polished house with the companionable air has all the markings of a well-bred manor home. Despite its European ancestry it is an American classic with great qualities. Its high style is purposely designed as a good fit for the neighborhood, for the other homes are comparable revival styles. Characterizing an earlier age and reflecting the success of Columbus's early businessmen and entrepreneurs, the neighborhood provides a fitting back-drop for Ohio's official governor's residence, just as the home itself offers a dignified refuge for Ohio's chief executive.

Living room with oak-paneled walls, molded plaster
ceiling, and leaded-glass doors flanking fireplace.

Close-up of front exterior, featuring front entry and lanterns.

Foyer featuring elegant walnut staircase and mahogany settee and stool in the "buckeye" design.

Front exterior showing decorative chimneys.

South Dakota
Governor's Mansion

National Register of Historic Places

Location: 119 North Washington, Pierre

Construction Year: 1936

Cost: $24,500

Size: 6,585 square feet

Number of Rooms: 14

Architect: Unknown (WPA Project)

Architectural Style: Modified Colonial

Furniture Style: Traditional

South Dakota is wonderfully exotic. The colorful names alone—Chief Red Cloud, Sitting Bull, Crazy Horse, General Custer—add drama to its history. Its identity is memorialized by the Battle of Little Big Horn, the precious archaeological resources in the Badlands, and the famous faces chiseled into the side of Mount Rushmore.

The romanticized frontier stereotype—fed by images of battles between the Sioux Nation and the white settlers, Teddy Roosevelt's hunting expeditions, and the gold rush in the Black Hills—can tell only part of the story. There is a variety found in South Dakota that challenges the common view that it is merely a vast empty land of harsh weather.

It is true that there is a huge openness to the land that makes the sky appear endless. And while the state is dry and looks barren, it is agriculturally productive and has great lakes created from large Missouri River dams. There are actually nine hundred square miles of water for recreation, and it is almost impossible to spot a car or truck without a boat hitch. On the eastern side of the Missouri River, which cuts the state vertically before angling toward the east, the state feels more midwestern and its rainfall is more abundant than on the western side of the state. The western region is where the state's mineral deposits are located. Mining operations extract valuable metallic minerals as well as deposits such as sand, gravel, and coal. The western part of the state is also a place of oil exploration and of sheep and cattle ranches.

One thing the Dakotas do not have is a burgeoning population. South Dakota, with a little over 750,000 people, has 90,000 more inhabitants than North Dakota. The surprise in the Dakotas is that "windswept" can go hand-in-hand with agricultural beauty—as seen alongside Highway 83, between Bismarck, North Dakota, and Pierre, South Dakota, where thousands and thousands of sunflowers, grown for their oil, spread as far as you can see. There are colorfully tinted rock layers and steep ravines in the Badlands, and thick forests of evergreen trees among the canyons and streams of the Black Hills.

The Dakota Territory, established in 1861, was a huge area including present-day North and South Dakota as well as large areas of Wyoming and Montana. The first capital was at Yankton, now in South Dakota, and the first territorial governor, William Jayne, was the personal friend and physician of President Abraham Lincoln.

By 1868, the Dakota Territory was rearranged by the establishment of other territories, causing it to become smaller, consisting of the Dakotas and a little area that later became part of Nebraska. Notwithstanding the Homestead Act of 1862, white settlement in the Dakotas was sparse. Enthusiasm for the promise of free land was held in check by the Civil War and skirmishes with the Sioux. After a treaty in 1868 calmed the Indian concerns, and after the arrival of the railroad in the 1870s, immigrants arrived from Scandinavia, Germany, and Eastern Europe. Miners and gold seekers pushed into the Black Hills, which had heretofore been Indian hunting and camping grounds.

In 1883, Territorial Governor Nehemiah Ordway moved the capital to Bismarck, in the northern region of the Dakota Territory. In response, South Dakota vigorously pursued statehood, which was finally granted in 1889 to both North and South Dakota. Pierre, located on the eastern bank of the Missouri River and near the center of the state, grew up where the railroad line stopped in 1880. The town was charted by the territorial government in 1883, and when statehood was declared, it was chosen as the temporary state capital. In the following year it gained permanent status, although there was another final vote in 1904 before making it official. Pierre should not be confused with its neighbor across the river, Fort Pierre, on the western bank at the juncture of the Missouri River and the Bad River, where Lewis and Clark had camped in 1804. Fort Pierre was the first permanent white settlement in South Dakota, having been the site of a trading post in 1817.

Legislative attempts to provide a residence for South Dakota's governors began in 1913, but no authorization was given until 1917, when the State Capitol Commission began a search. In 1920, a large tract of land was purchased next to Capitol Lake, and an existing simple cottage on the property was used for the residence until a new house was erected in 1936. For more than thirty years, South Dakota's governors had received a monthly housing allowance and had chosen their own places to live—some in houses and others in hotels.

Recognizing that the small bungalow was inadequate, but lacking the legislative support necessary to build a new governor's mansion, Governor Tom Berry obtained a commitment from the Works Progress Administration (WPA) to build it with federal money. The new governor's residence was constructed, during the Great Depression, on the same property as the original house. The original cottage was sold for $1,279 and moved to another location.

The WPA, started in 1935, was one of President Franklin D. Roosevelt's relief agencies created during the Depression; it provided jobs by building public projects such as bridges, streets, and highways. South Dakota is unique in having the only governor's mansion in the United States built by the WPA. Historian Harold H. Schuler noted that "Thirty-five men were provided employment for over a year during 1935–1936" when the home was constructed.[1]

The completed house is a two-story simplified colonial home, built from native materials and containing fourteen rooms and four fireplaces—three of the fireplaces were made from petrified wood. The house and its grounds are on the east side of Capitol Lake, and the property adjoins the capitol grounds. Looking beyond the ten-acre lake, one sees the beautiful dark dome of the limestone Classical Revival style–capitol building.

Over the years, the space in the house has been reconfigured; for example, in the 1960s, the original garage was converted into additional living space. It is now a family room that can also be used for an office. The changes to the house have not been drastic, however. The original white exterior siding was painted gray during the administration of Governor and Mrs. Joseph Foss (1955–1959). Despite the addition of white shutters and corrugated awnings, the house continues to be representative of its lineage and is in complete accord with its earlier look.

The governor's mansion is in the middle of four and a half well-tended acres that are encircled by a walking path and a long front circle drive. It is a beautiful property, planted with flow-

1. Harold H. Schuler, *Pierre since 1910*, 27.

ers, shrubbery, and very old trees. The view of Capitol Lake is especially interesting because of all that it contains. First there is the reflection of the capitol building in the lake, and then there are the waterfowl—ducks and Canada geese that migrate there because the lake is fed by warm artesian well water and never completely freezes. On the shores of the lake is a flaming fountain, a veterans' memorial, that has burned since the mid-1960s when the well water, with its high concentration of natural gas, was first ignited. The flame is not very visible during the day, but at night it glows blue and orange.

In 1970, when Governor and Mrs. Frank Farrar occupied the house, a teakwood panel from a plank on the *USS South Dakota* was donated to the mansion to decorate the fireplace in the reception room, which at that time was the formal room for entertaining official visitors to the house. In 1994, this space was converted to become the present formal dining room, and the teak panel is now in the museum of the South Dakota State Historical Society.

In September 1976, the governor's mansion was listed on the National Register of Historic Places. Since then, all work done on the residence has been subject to the approval of the Capitol Complex Restoration and Beautification Commission. The separate garage, built in the 1980s, looks as if it has always been there. In 1993, eighty-three thousand dollars was spent to repaint and renovate the residence. This included tearing out and replacing concrete floors for a complicated furnace installation. A very large patio has been added to the exterior, and a berm was built up on the rear of the property to allow for more privacy.

The residence was planned for the governor's private use as well as for official entertaining, and it continues to be used for these purposes today. The interior of the house does not accommodate large groups, and the house is not open for public tours.

South Dakota's monuments commemorate the famous and powerful individuals as well as the Indian and the farmer. Of course there are monuments to Lewis and Clark and their famous expedition, but all the other historical markers and monuments call to mind remarkable accomplishments in the unfolding of South Dakota's and the country's history.

A book written in 1932 suggested that events that occurred in South Dakota and contributed to its rich heritage would one day be commemorated by historical markers, just as in the East:

> When you travel through some of our older eastern states, you will pass along highways that are near the scenes of important events; frequently by the roadside will be seen a tablet—a marker—which will tell the story of what took place. It may be the birthplace of some noted American, or the site of the making of some useful invention, or the site of a battle or a first settlement. What would you think of some such marked highway in South Dakota? You may say that our state is not old enough to have much history to tell about. That may be true; it is also true that we do not care so much about places and their meanings when we are near them and can see them. But when we cannot see them every day, they seem to mean more.[2]

2. Ralph V. Hunkins and John Clark Lindsey, *South Dakota: Its Past, Present, and Future*, 300.

Today, South Dakota's great open terrain no longer lacks markers observing its history. In the capitol complex alone, where hundreds of trees shade Hilger's Gulch Park, next to the capitol, there are twenty-eight monuments dedicated to former governors. Nearby, a granite veterans' memorial honors the war dead, this, in turn, not far from the flame of the fountain in Capitol Lake. From the Fort Pierre Memorial and the governor's mansion grounds to the gigantic Crazy Horse Memorial carved from a granite mountain, South Dakota honors the contributions of its people and celebrates their memory.

Front entrance of the South
Dakota governor's residence.

A martin box shows the practical side of lakefront living.

Living room. *Photograph by Chad Coppess, South Dakota Department of Tourism.*

Dining room. *Photograph by Chad Coppess, South Dakota Department of Tourism.*

Wisconsin
Governor's Mansion

Location: 99 Cambridge Road, Madison

Construction Year: 1928

Cost: $49,500*

Size: 16,000 square feet

Number of Rooms: 34

Architect: Frank Riley

Architectural Style: Classical Revival

Furniture Style: Georgian Antiques and Reproductions

* Cost to state when purchased in 1949; there is no known record
of the original cost to build.

While geology created a high green isthmus resting atop the blue lakes of Wisconsin, it took a country judge with a hefty political will to transform the Four Lakes region into a historic landmark. An 1828 exploring trip through the sleeping Wisconsin wilderness forever changed the direction of Judge James Duane Doty's life and that of the quiet landscape crisscrossed by soft Indian paths. Convinced this property should become the site of the future capital of the future Wisconsin Territory, the persistent Doty shook it from its slumber and pushed it toward its destiny while bestowing on it an important role in a restless new era of noise and progress.

Barely waiting for the ink to dry on his newly done survey, Doty marched to the legislature in 1834, armed with facts and figures to substantiate his claims that this property would be the best of the nineteen locations then under discussion as potential sites. In 1836 Congress granted Wisconsin its own territorial status, and Doty sold his vision to the legislators through a combination of outright promotion and sentimental appeal. Doty presented to them his plans for a city, which he named Madison after the ever-popular and recently deceased president. He even went so far as to lay out the future streets leading to the capitol on diagonals, following the same concept used by the architect L'Enfant in laying out Washington, D.C. Furthermore, he proposed names for the streets, in honor of the signers of the U.S. Constitution.

Early on, Doty had accumulated the land where he envisioned his Madison creation would be located. Within a few days after the legislature had approved the Madison capital site, Doty, in a gesture of appreciation, offered the lawmakers some of the choicest lots at very favorable prices.

It was amid speculation that Doty bribed the legislators, successfully converting the Indian campground on the banks of Lakes Mendota and Monona into the site for the city of Madison. In 1841, Doty was appointed the second territorial governor of the Wisconsin Territory.

Although Doty later served in Congress, was appointed superintendent of Indian Affairs, and became governor of the Utah Territory, he is most vividly remembered as the controversial politician and land speculator who gave his heart and soul to politics while maintaining his livelihood with high-powered land deals, uppermost of which was his buying and selling of the land for the Wisconsin territorial capital.

And while it is true that within the next four years he was successful in masterminding the outcome of the capital location, there was an aftermath of resentment that crippled his future political ability. As governor, Doty was unable to unite voters behind his proposals for statehood. Henry Dodge, who had been the first territorial governor, was reappointed to that office in 1845 as the third governor, and it was during his tenure that statehood finally came to Wisconsin.

It was not until many years later that any meaningful activity concerning a governor's residence took place in the state. Such activity began with Governor Jeremiah McLain Rusk, who became the state's fourteenth governor, serving from 1881 until 1889. Unlike Governor Doty, who could trace his ancestry back to the *Mayflower*, Governor Rusk had an unpretentious family background. His father was poor and died young, and as a youth, Rusk—having little formal education—had supported himself as a farmer and a stagecoach driver. Governor Rusk's prolific career covered everything from tavern operator to sheriff, to Civil War general, and eventually to United States Secretary of Agriculture.

In 1881, as governor, Rusk purchased a house built in 1854 by a wealthy citizen, Julius T. White, who was Governor Doty's brother-in-law. White had built the house on land originally owned by James Doty. The dignified square brown house was built on the bank overlooking Lake Mendota, and the site was shaded by oak, elm, and maple trees. The house contained two stories and had a mansard roof, a veranda, and a second-floor balustrade that was supported by Corinthian columns; it combined a number of classical styles. Built of local brown sandstone, it was nevertheless called the "White House," for it was owned by a family named White. In those days in Madison, houses were not given street addresses, but were identified by the original owner's name or by their location in reference to a known building, such as a church or a hotel.

As Governor Rusk's term of office was coming to a close, he urged the state to purchase the White House from him so it could be used as the official governor's mansion; he offered it to the state for twenty thousand dollars, and Wisconsin purchased the home. This august historic home with windows ten feet high served as the official residence for the Wisconsin's governors for sixty-three years.

Although the house began showing its age, it continued to be a source of pride for the state of Wisconsin. In the early 1930s, Governor and Mrs. Walter J. Kohler were the occupants of the residence. Mrs. Kohler valued the eighty-year-old house and succeeded in restoring its antique interior; displaying tremendous foresight for historic preservation, she stressed the importance of "bringing it all back to the old."[1]

Despite the efforts of the Kohlers and their immediate successors, Governor and Mrs. Phillip LaFollette, to preserve the mansion, it eventually became clear that the house was no longer serviceable. When Governor Oscar Rennebohm took office in 1947, he discovered that the venerable old building was also cold and drafty. It inefficiently served the governor's needs: The private area of the house was not large enough for the family to have overnight company and still maintain a sense of privacy, and it was plainly awkward for the governor and his family to share a bathroom with important overnight guests. At Governor Rennebohm's urging, the state wasted little time and in 1949 purchased the present residence located on Cambridge Road.

In 1921, the Wisconsin industrialist Carl A. Johnson began building the Cambridge Road house that would eventually become the Wisconsin governor's residence. While construction was under way, his wife died, and Carl Johnson had the house boarded up. It remained unfinished until he remarried in 1928 and completed the house. He later sold it to Thomas R. Hefty, a Madison banker, who sold it to the state in 1949 for only $49,500—a quarter of its assessed value of $200,000. When the state acquired the house, it had been vacant for several years and required renovation work to make it liveable.

The elegant, solidly built residence, situated on four and a half acres on the western banks of large Lake Mendota, was created by the Wisconsin architect Frank Riley, who designed other

1. *The Wisconsin State Journal*, June 22, 1930. See also John Drury, *Historic Midwest Houses*.

expensive Wisconsin homes of that time. A grand and mighty house built of white-painted sandstone and topped with a copper roof, it almost seems to rise from the water. On the street side of the home is a bold, beautiful, and antique wrought-iron fence that had once surrounded the old state capitol building. The governor's residence is located in the village of Maple Bluff, a suburb on the north shore of Madison that was once a Native American campground; the Winnebago had many summertime encampments here. Some of the nearby homes, like the governor's residence, are built on the water's edge and have sweeping views and impressive entrances, but few are as stately and monumental as the governor's residence.

One can see Lake Mendota from the front door of the residence. Beyond the lake, one sees the dome of the magnificent state capitol, built in the Classical Revival style and modeled after the U.S. Capitol in Washington, D.C.

The Wisconsin governor's residence is also Classical Revival; in keeping with that style, it has an immense, two-story, six-column Doric portico that, along with a grand approach and entrance, remind one of the White House. Inside, the house has sixteen thousand square feet of living space and thirty-four rooms.

To enter the residence, one walks up a few steps and crosses the portico to the front door. Stepping into the entryway, one's view straight ahead is of the unusually large foyer and into the reception room beyond. Four classical columns flank the wide entrance to the reception room, which is decorated with antiques from England, Italy, China, and Portugal. The foyer is framed with an elaborate double staircase: two symmetrical stairways, one on each side of the foyer. Passing underneath the staircase makes the ceiling seem incredibly high and the foyer look even more opulent. The oversized foyer easily accommodates furnishings that include an 1820s French fainting couch, a circa-1800 secretary, two console tables, and armchairs. The bronze chandelier is a copy of a 1900 lantern and a replica of the one hanging in the White House foyer in Washington, D.C.

The drawing room is the formal "entertaining" room of the house. It features its original oak floor as well as a more recent hand-carved pine mantelpiece. The room is furnished with a combination of period pieces and reproductions. When less formality is desirable, the more intimate library is used for entertaining. Its solid furnishings include an antique Italian mantelpiece of Sienna marble, walnut paneling, a leather sofa, and durable wooden tables. Bookcases line the library walls; the walnut paneling has been pegged to the wall using no nails.

The Classical Revival style follows antique architectural forms traced to Rome and Greece rather than to the religious roots of the Gothic style or to the colonial roots of America in the 1700s. But the term *Classical Revival* can be a source of confusion because, in addition to Roman and Greek Revival, the term is also used to refer to the Federal, Neoclassical, and Jeffersonian styles. Revival styles of foreign ancestry were popular in America between 1890 and 1940.

Governor Warren P. Knowles, elected in 1964, served three terms. Upon taking office, Governor and Mrs. Knowles launched a massive plan to recondition the governor's mansion. Little had been done since the purchase and initial renovation in 1949. Mrs. Knowles described the situation: "The place was a fire-trap . . . we were afraid to move in."[2] Apparently she did not overstate the situation. The house needed more than mere decorating.

With devotion and determination, Dorothy Knowles raised the standards for renovation by initiating and leading a total restoration. She made two trips to Washington, D.C., in order to observe and follow the example earlier set by First Lady Jacqueline Kennedy in the White House renovation. Because Mrs. Knowles so immersed herself in the Wisconsin mansion project, all of the renovation work was done according to a plan, and nothing was done in a piece-meal way.

One hundred years after the death of Governor Doty, Mrs. Knowles also had a project to sell to the state lawmakers. She went to the legislature armed with her recommendations for fixing the ills of the governor's mansion. And just as Doty's plan to make Madison the capital in the territorial days succeeded, Mrs. Knowles's project also met with success. She asked the legislature for an appropriation to put the mansion in order and promised to create a tax-free vehicle for receiving contributions; thus the Wisconsin Executive Residence Foundation, Inc., was born. The Wisconsin legislature appropriated $248,000 to repair and replace the antiquated infrastructure of the house, and Mrs. Knowles solicited an additional $30,000 from individuals to complete the interior decorating. During the year-long renovation, the Knowles family resided in the old governor's mansion at 130 East Gilman Street. Today, the old residence is still standing and is used as a student dormitory for the University of Wisconsin.

Mrs. Knowles recruited the university's Horticultural and Landscaping Department to develop the mansion grounds. More recently, during Governor and Mrs. Tommy Thompson's residency in the mansion, several of the garden spaces were completed and dedicated, reflecting their interest in the property. Today the landscaping features several formal and informal gardens with both perennials and annuals, a cutting garden, an herb garden, and a fragrance garden. The generous use of trees and shrubs defines the space and gives a sense of order. Within the garden are flowering trees, a fountain, ornamental fencing, and vine-covered entrances; during the growing season, the mansion grounds are bedecked with color.

A majority of the mansion's furnishings are eighteenth-century antiques and reproductions. Several pieces were brought from the old governor's residence, while others have been acquired over the years by the Wisconsin Executive Residence Foundation. In order to maintain consistency for the interior and the exterior of the residence, the State Capitol and Executive Board was created. It oversees and monitors all changes, repairs, and additions to the building and its furnishings.

Among the fine eighteenth-century English antiques found in the house are a satinwood game table, a Hepplewhite love seat, a Sheraton settee that once belonged to the Earl of Lowther Castle, and a pair of decorated Hepplewhite armchairs. There are nineteenth-century furnishings, as well, such as a gilt French Empire floor-to-ceiling pier mirror, which is orig-

2. Quoted in Nancy Greenwood Williams, *First Ladies of Wisconsin: The Governors' Wives*, 218.

inal to the house, and a secretary that was moved from the old house and now greets guests in the foyer. In the dining room is a late Georgian style mahogany server from the old executive residence. In addition to the numerous antiques, there are quality reproductions including a pine mantelpiece in the drawing room that replicates an eighteenth-century English design.

This strong, beautiful house gives the impression that it will endure for centuries. Although it is the temporary home for governors and their families, there is nothing temporary in the look of the building. Its history, atmosphere, and environment give it a permanent place in Wisconsin's future.

The daily operation and maintenance of the mansion is a big production. It is managed with great devotion by an efficient and caring group of individuals. The property seems to glow with all the attention it receives from its full-time staff, its volunteers, and from personnel from the University of Wisconsin. Weekly tours are given by volunteer docents, and gardening services continue to be provided by the Horticultural and Landscaping Department of the university.

From the early years, when James Doty drew plans and named streets for a capital city of the future, to today, Madison's history can be glimpsed through architecture. The builders of the capital city expressed their state pride through the symmetry, proportion, and orderliness of Classical architecture used in the capitol building and first and present governors' mansions, and renovators have continued that tradition of pride. The governor's mansion—symbolizing the successful history of Wisconsin, a story that binds together early Wisconsin characters like James Doty and Jeremiah Rusk with later ones like Oscar Rennebohm and Dorothy Knowles— is a historic location that first gave shelter to early Indian settlers and now showcases Wisconsin's prosperity and deep heritage.

Ornate wrought-iron fencing was brought
from the old capitol building.

The Wisconsin governor's mansion rests
serenely by Lake Mendota.

The foyer, the chandelier like that in the White House, the double staircase, and the antique fainting couch.

Living room windows offer views
of the gardens and Lake Mendota.

Front exterior view featuring two-story columns.

Powder room with ornate gilded pier mirror and
amethyst chandelier. Both were in the house before
it was purchased by the state.

One of the gardens, with gazebo and pergola.

Bibliography

Newspapers

Indiana

Indianapolis News, January 2, 1909; March 3, 1916; July 7, 1961; February 19, 1969; November 2, 1969; June 6, 1973; July 7, 1973; July 27, 1973; September 15, 1973; June 12, 1975.

Indianapolis Star, December 21, 1952; March 15, 1964; April 12, 1964; May 3, 1964; January 13, 1969; August 27, 1971; August 5, 1973; June 15, 1975; June 20, 1982; January 2, 1984; April 1, 1984.

Tri-State Trader, November 6, 1976.

Illinois

Illinois State Journal, June 28, 1936; October 10, 1955; October 12, 1955; October 13, 1955; October 14, 1955; October 17, 1955; October 21, 1955; October 26, 1955; May 29, 1963.

Illinois State Journal-Register, November 8, 1931; 1933 (no month); January 1, 1940; April 29, 1941; October 29, 1941; November 10, 1948; December 30, 1951; April 16, 1955; November 23, 1955; December 21, 1955; October 14, 1956; June 10, 1965; January 28, 1968; December 1, 1972; December 16, 1988.

Illinois State Register, October 11, 1955; October 12, 1955; October 17, 1955; March 19, 1860.

Iowa

Des Moines Register, January 26, 1969; 1970, (no month); August 24, 1971; June 20, 1972; September 17, 1972; October 9, 1972; June 24, 1973; July 14, 1973; July 7, 1974; 1974 (no month).

Kansas

Daily Capital, undated (about 1955).

Fort Scott Tribune, September 7, 1982.

Hutchinson News, September 11 and 27, 1986; December 28, 1986.

Kansas City Star, November 25, 1945; January 27, 1957.

Kansas City Times, February 14, 1963; October 30, 1963; February 18, 1965; February 29, 1984; May 27, 1987.

Kansas Democrat, January 21, 1889.

Lawrence Journal World, October 10, 1982.

Olathe Daily News, January 11, 1980.

Topeka Capital Journal, April 27, 1937; October 14, 1955; November 18, 1955; January 19, 1956; April 11, 1957; June 13, 1957; July 15, 1957; July 31, 1957; August 29, 1957; October 10, 27, 1957; April 4, 24, 1959; April 28, 1961; April 22, 1962; March 26, 1963; June 19, 21, 1963; November 1, 1964; June 19, 1965; May 16, 18, 1975; October 8, 1981; December 12, 1982; April 20, 1984.

Topeka State Journal, January 14, 1919; May 30, 1937; October 24, 1947; June 20, 1955; November 17, 1955; January 4, 1956; February 27, 1957; June 6, 1957.

Wichita Eagle-Beacon, January 29, 1981; September 25, 1982.

Wichita Eagle Magazine section, January 22, 1956.

Wichita Morning Eagle, August 14, 1961.

Michigan

Ann Arbor News, July 23, 1955.

Bay City Times, July 11, 1955.

Detroit Free Press, January 27, 1954; November 28, 1968; March 12, 1969, March 13, 1969; April 19, 1969; July 13, 1970; July 11, 1971; December 11, 1972; June 23, 1983; July 16, 1983; November 27, 1972; May 13, 1973; March 9, 1975.

Detroit News, March 20, 1962; December 29, 1964; September 5, 1982; June 24, 1984.

Flint Journal, July 11, 1955.

Grand Rapids Press, May 26, 1955.

Hastings Banner, April 25, 1968.

Kalamazoo Gazette, March 13, 1955.

Lansing State Journal, September 21, 1948.

Milwaukee Sentinel, September 28, 1966.

New York Times, July 8, 1973; June 29, 1997.

Saginaw News, January 7, 1951.

State Journal, January 19, 1947; March 13, 1955; April 28, 1955; May 20, 1955; May 24, 1955; July 3, 1955; July 22, 1955; December 11, 1956; May 17, 1959; December 29, 1964; January 12, 1966. March 21, 1966; November 27, 1968; February 9, 1969; July 1, 1969; August 20, 1969; January 12, 1970.

St. Louis Post-Dispatch, January 25, 2000.

Minnesota

Minneapolis Star, May 22, 1965; May 31, 1968.
St. Paul Dispatch, September 6, 1965.
St. Paul Pioneer Press, 1965; January 11, 1966; October 26, 1967; January 3, 1971; July 5, 1973;
 August 8, 1980.

Missouri

Kansas City Star, January 28, 1962.
St. Louis Globe Democrat, April 29, 1945; May 1, 1955; March 31, 1962; August 3, 1969;
 November 27, 1969; June 8, 1975.
St. Louis Post-Dispatch, December 25, 1887; February 25, 1945; October 21, 1963.

North Dakota

Bismarck-Manden Shopper, April 21, 1960.
Bismarck Tribune, February 21, 1951; April 18, 1958, April 16, 1958; April 16, 1960; December
 23, 1975; January 22, 1982; May 24, 1985.
Denver Post, October 17, 1952.
Fargo Forum, February 25, 1951; April 24, 1960; September 8, 1985.
St. Louis Post-Dispatch, August 20, 1995; December 19, 1996.

Nebraska

Denver Post, October 1952.
Lincoln Journal, August 20, 1956.
Lincoln Star, November 12, 1957; February 1958.
Lincoln Sunday Journal and Star, August 5, 1956; August 19, 1956; September 22, 1957; March
 6, 1997, March 26, 1997.
Lincoln Sunday Star, June 8, 1924.
Nebraska State Journal, June 1899; March 20, 1974.
Omaha World-Herald, 1954 or 1955; August 26, 1956; August 4, 1957; March 16, 1958; March
 1, 1992.

Ohio

Columbus Citizen-Journal, May 31, 1983.
Akron Beacon Journal, March 18, 1984.

South Dakota

Huron Daily Plainsman, January 18, 1970.
Pierre Daily Capitol Journal, February 23, 1963.
Sioux Falls Argus-Leader, January 16, 1955; July 14, 1993.
Watertown South Dakota Public Opinion, January 14, 1970.

Wisconsin

Capital Times, April 10, 1932.
St. Louis Post-Dispatch, May 3, 1998.
Milwaukee Sentinel, December 26, 1920.
Minneapolis Journal, May 31, 1893.
New York Times, October 31, 1999.
Wisconsin State Journal, June 4, 1922; March 2, 1930; June 22, 1930; October 16, 1968.

Brochures and Pamphlets

Illinois Governor's Residence (brochures during Edgar administration).
Heritage Museum of Kappa Kappa Gamma Fraternity (brochure).
Nebraska Governor's Residence (brochure during Nelson administration).
Nelson, Diane. *Nebraska Governor's Residence: Tour of the Restoration Project,* 1998.
North Dakota Governor's Residence (brochures during administrations of Governors Guy, Link, and Schafer).
North Dakota Inventory of Historic Places. February 15, 1977.
North Dakota's Former Governors' Mansion (commemorative centennial booklet), August 1, 1993.
Ohio Governor's Residence (brochure during Taft administration).
Ohio Governor's Residence (brochure during Voinovich administration).
Peterson, Eugene. *Historic Mackinac Island Visitor's Guide.* Mackinac State Historic Parks, 1994.
South Dakota Governor's Residence (brochure during the Mickelson administration).
Terrace Hill Society. *The Historic Governors Mansion* (brochure).
Terrace Hill Society. *Terrace Hill . . . Iowa's Historic Governors Mansion,* educational guide (brochure).
Wilson, D. Ray. *Iowa Historical Tour Guide.* Carpentersville, Ill.: Crossroads Communication, 1986.
Wisconsin Executive Residence Foundation (brochure), 1969.

References

Adams, Hermoine van Laer. "The Governor's Mansion, 1901–1962." *Bulletin of the Shawnee County Historical Society* 39 (summer 1963): 2–8.

Andrews, Wayne. *Architecture, Ambition, and Americans: A Social History of American Architecture.* Rev. ed. New York: Free Press, 1978.

Baker, Patricia D., "The Governor's Residence." Macalester College, St. Paul, Minn., May 1980. Governor's Residence file, Minnesota State Historical Society.

Bald, F. Clever. *Michigan in Four Centuries: Line Drawings by William Thomas Woodward.* New York: Harper and Brothers, Publishers, 1954.

Blegan, Theodore C. *Grass Roots History.* Minneapolis: University of Minnesota Press, 1947.

——— . *Minnesota: A History of the State.* Minneapolis: University of Minnesota Press, 1963.

Bodenhamer, David J., Lamont Hulse, and Elizabeth B. Monroe. *The Main Stem: The History and Architecture of North Meridian Street.* Indianapolis: Historic Landmarks Foundation of Indiana, 1992.

Boorstin, Daniel J. *The Americans: The National Experience.* New York: Random House, 1965.

Bray, Robert C. *Rediscoveries: Literature and Place in Illinois.* Urbana: University of Illinois Press, 1982.

Briggs, Harold E. *Frontiers of the Northwest: A History of the Upper Missouri Valley.* New York: D. Appleton-Century, 1940.

Brooks, H. Allen. *Frank Lloyd Wright and the Prairie School.* New York: George Braziller, 1984.

Bruccoli, Matthew J. *Some Sort of Epic Grandeur: The Life of F. Scott Fitzgerald.* New York: Harcourt Brace Jovanovich Publishers, 1981.

Bryan, John Albury. *Missouri's Contribution to American Architecture: A History of the Architectural Achievements in This State from the Time of the Earliest Settlements down to the Present Year.* St. Louis: St. Louis Architectural Club, 1928.

Buisseret, David. *Historic Illinois from the Air.* Chicago: University of Chicago Press, 1990.

Burchard, John, and Albert Bush-Brown. *Architecture of America: A Social and Cultural History.* Boston: Little, Brown, 1961.

Campden, Richard N. *Ohio: An Architectural Portrait.* Chagrin Falls: West Summit Press and Richard N. Campden, 1973.

Carley, Rachel. *The Visual Dictionary of American Domestic Architecture.* New York: Henry Holt, 1994.

Carrier, Lois A. *Illinois: Crossroads of a Continent.* Urbana: University of Illinois Press, 1993.

Cathcart, Charlotte. *Indianapolis from Our Old Corner.* Indianapolis: Indiana Historical Society and Studio Press, 1965.

Catton, Bruce. *Michigan: A Bicentennial History.* New York: Norton, 1976.

Christensen, Lawrence O., and Gary R. Kremer. *A History of Missouri: Volume IV, 1875 to 1919.* Columbia: University of Missouri Press, 1997.

Christensen, Trilby Busch. "Looking a Gift Horse in the Mouth." *Twin Cities,* July 1982, 38–47, 70–81.

Christman, Margaret C. S. *1846: Portrait of the Nation.* Washington, D.C: Smithsonian Institution Press, 1996.

Coleman, Nadine Mills. *Mistress of Ravenswood.* Columbia, Mo. : Tribune Publishing, 1992.

Cooley, Thomas McIntyre. *Michigan: A History of Governments.* American Commonwealths. Boston: Houghton, Mifflin, 1889.

Corneau, Octavia Roberts. *Mansion Memories.* 1956.

Creigh, Dorothy Weyer. *Nebraska: A Bicentennial History.* New York: Norton, 1977.

Culmer, Frederick Arthur. *A New History of Missouri.* Mexico, Mo.: McIntyre Publishers, 1938.

Current, Richard Nelson. *Wisconsin: A Bicentennial History.* New York: Norton, 1977.

Dahl, Orrin L. *Des Moines: Capital City.* Tulsa: Continental Heritage, 1978.

Daniel, Jean Houston, and Price Daniel. *Executive Mansions and Capitols of America.* Waukesha, Wis.: Country Beautiful, 1969.

Davis, Kenneth S. *Kansas: A Bicentennial History.* New York: Norton, 1976.

Devlin, Harry. *Portraits of American Architecture: A Gallery of Victorian Homes.* 2d ed. New York: Gramercy Books, 1996.

Drache, Hiram M. *The Day of the Bonanza: A History of Bonanza Farming in the Red River Valley of the North.* Danville, Ill.: Interstate Printers and Publishers, 1964.

"Dragon in the Mansion." *The Beta Theta Pi,* March 1963, 3–4.

Drury, John. *Historic Midwest Houses.* Minneapolis: University of Minnesota Press, 1947.

———. *Old Illinois Houses.* Springfield: Illinois State Historical Society, 1941.

Dunbar, Willis Frederick. *Michigan: A History of the Wolverine State.* Grand Rapids, Mich.: William B. Eerdmans Publishing, 1970.

Eckert, Kathryn Bishop. *Buildings of Michigan.* New York: Oxford University Press, 1993.

Elazar, Daniel J. *Cities of the Prairie: The Metropolitan Frontier and American Politics.* New York: Basic Books, 1970.

Elstein, Rochelle S. "The Howard Sober House: Artifact of the 1950s." *Magazine of the Historical Society of Michigan* 16, no. 3 (fall 1980): 4–8.

Executive Mansion. Ohio Archeological and Historical Society Publications, n.d. In Governor's Residence file, Ohio Historical Society.

Facts about the Recently Completed Repair and Renovation of Cedar Crest, the Executive Mansion for the State of Kansas, October 21, 1975. [Tour guide information.] Governor's Mansion file, Kansas Historical Society.

Faulkner, Virginia. *Roundup: A Nebraska Reader.* Lincoln: University of Nebraska Press, 1957.

Federal Writers' Project. *Illinois: A Descriptive and Historical Guide.* American Guide Series. Chicago: A. C. McClurg, 1939.

———. *North Dakota: A Guide to the Northern Prairie State.* New York: Oxford University Press, 1950.

Foley, Mary Mix. *The American House.* New York: Harper and Row, 1980.

Foley, William E. *The Genesis of Missouri: From Wilderness Outpost to Statehood.* Columbia: University of Missouri Press, 1989.

———. *A History of Missouri: Volume I, 1673 to 1820.* Columbia: University of Missouri Press, 1971.

Folmar, John Kent. *This State of Wonders: The Letters of an Iowa Frontier Family, 1858–1861.* Iowa City: University of Iowa Press, 1986.

Gebhard, David, and Gerald Mansheim. *Buildings of Iowa.* New York: Oxford University Press, 1993.

Giffen, Jerena East. *First Ladies of Missouri: Their Homes and Their Families.* Rev. ed. Jefferson City: Giffen Enterprises, 1996.

Gilpin, Alec R. *The Territory of Michigan (1805–1837).* Lansing: Michigan State University Press, 1970.

Goettsch, Scherrie, and Steve Weinberg. *Terrace Hill: The Story of a House and the People Who Touched It.* Des Moines, Iowa: Wallace-Homestead, 1979.

Governor's Residence File, Minnesota Historical Society.

Gowans, Alan. *Images of American Living: Four Centuries of Architecture and Furniture as Cultural Expression.* Philadelphia: J. B. Lippincott, 1964.

———. *Styles and Types of North American Architecture: Social Function and Cultural Expression.* New York: Icon Editions, 1992.

Hager, Dorothy. *First Ladies of North Dakota.* Minot, N.D.: North Dakota Secretarial Service, 1967.

Hahn, Ralph, and Associates. Report of Structural Investigation, Executive Mansion, March 16, 1970.

Halda, Bonnie. "Research and Restoration of Former Governor's Mansion." *North Dakota History,* spring 1980.

Hall, James Dorsett. "Cedar Crest: A Case for Its Historic Preservation." Law School requirement, University of Kansas, 1981.

Hammett, Ralph W. *Architecture in the United States: A Survey of Architectural Styles since 1776.* New York: John Wiley and Sons, 1976.

Handlin, David P. *American Architecture.* London: Thames and Hudson, 1985.

Harlan, Edgar Rubey. *A Narrative History of the People of Iowa. . . .* Volume 1. Chicago: American Historical Society, 1931.

Harris, Cyril M. *American Architecture: An Illustrated Encyclopedia.* New York: Norton, 1998.

Havighurst, Walter. *Ohio: A Bicentennial History.* New York: Norton, 1976.

Heidenreich, Virginia L., ed. *North Dakota's Former Governors' Mansion: Its History and Presentation.* Bismarck: State Historical Society of North Dakota, 1991.

Hitchcock, Henry-Russell. *Architecture: Nineteenth and Twentieth Century.* London: Penguin Group, 1989.

Hodges, Layra Fletcher. *Early Indianapolis.* Indianapolis: C. E. Pauley, vol. 7, no. 5, 1919.

Holloway, W. R. *Indianapolis: A Historical and Statistical Sketch. . . .* Indianapolis: Indianapolis

Journal Print, 1870.

"Home for Minnesota's Governor," *Gopher Historian,* spring 1966, 12–17.

"Houseful of History: The Executive Mansion." *Dispatch* [Illinois State Historical Society], June, August, and October, 1972.

Howard, Hugh. *The Preservationist's Progress: Architectural Adventures in Conserving Yesterday's Houses.* New York: Farrar, Straus and Giroux, 1991.

Howard, Robert P. *Illinois: A History of the Prairie State.* Grand Rapids, Mich.: William B. Eerdmans Publishing, 1975.

——— . *Mostly Good and Competent Men.* Springfield, Ill.: Illinois Issues, Sagamon State University, and Illinois State Historical Society, 1988.

Howe, Henry. *Historical Collections of Ohio* 1 (1902). Cincinnati: C. J. Krehbiel.

Hunkins, Ralph V., and John Clark Lindsey. *South Dakota: Its Past, Present, and Future.* New York: Macmillan, 1932.

Hunt, William Dudley, Jr. *Encyclopedia of American Architecture.* New York: McGraw-Hill, 1980.

Ierley, Merritt. *Open House: A Guided Tour of the American Home, 1637–Present.* New York: Henry Holt, 1999.

Illinois Division of Architecture and Engineering. Report on Executive Mansion. Springfield, Ill., March 1, 1965.

Illinois Executive Mansion Commission. Building Subcommittee Report, December, 1966.

Illinois Executive Mansion Commission. Report to Illinois General Assembly, with Recommendations for Action, March 1967.

Jensen, Richard J. *Illinois: A Bicentennial History.* New York: Norton, 1978.

Journal of the Illinois State Historical Society 36 (1943): 41–49.

Junior League of Lincoln, Nebraska. *An Architectural Album.* Lincoln, Nebr.: The League, 1979.

Kemp, Jim. *American Vernacular: Regional Influences in Architecture and Interior Design.* New York: Viking, 1987.

Kennedy, Roger. *Minnesota Houses: An Architectural and Historical Overview.* Minneapolis: Dillon Press, 1967.

Kidney, Walter C. *Historic Buildings of Ohio.* Pittsburgh: Ober Park Associates, 1972.

Kimball, Fiske. *American Architecture.* Indianapolis: Bobbs-Merrill, 1928.

King, Rufus. *Ohio: First Fruits of the Ordinance of 1787.* Boston: Houghton Mifflin, 1888.

Koupal, Nancy Tystad, ed. "Lydia Norbeck's Recollections of the Years," 1978.

Krohe, James, Jr., ed. *A Springfield Reader: Historical Views of the Illinois Capital, 1818–1976.* Springfield, Ill.: Sangamon County Historical Society, 1976.

LaFollette, Isabel Bacon. "Early History of the Wisconsin Executive Residence." *Wisconsin Magazine of History,* no. 21 (December 1937): 138–50.

Lamar, Howard R. *Dakota Territory, 1861–1889.* New Haven: Yale University Press, 1956.

Lass, William E. *Minnesota: A Bicentennial History.* New York: Norton, 1977.

Leary, Edward A. *Indianapolis: The Story of a City.* Indianapolis: Bobbs-Merrill, 1970.

Letters from Paulen, Landon, Schoeppel, Carlson, and Avery administrations. Governor's

Mansion files, Kansas Historical Society.

LeVander, Iantha Powrie. Papers, 1962–1990. Minnesota Historical Society.

Low, Ann Marie. *Dust Bowl Diary*. Lincoln: University of Nebraska Press, 1984.

Madison, James H., ed. *Heartland: Comparative Histories of the Midwestern States*. Bloomington: Indiana University Press, 1990.

"The Mansion Has Seen Changes Inside and Out." *Society for the Preservation of the Governor's Mansion Newsletter* 1, no. 1 (spring 1979): 142.

March, David D. *The History of Missouri*. Volume 2. New York: Lewis Historical Publishing, 1967.

Margolis, Jon. "The Reopening of the Frontier." *New York Times Magazine,* October 15, 1995.

Martin, John Bartlow. *Indiana: An Interpretation*. New York: Alfred A. Knopf, 1947.

McAlester, Virginia, and Lee McAlester. *A Field Guide to American Houses*. New York: Alfred A. Knopf, 1984.

———. *A Field Guide to America's Historic Neighborhoods and Museum Houses*. New York: Alfred A. Knopf, 1998.

———. *Great American Houses and Their Architectural Styles*. New York: Abbeville Press, 1994.

McCandless, Perry. *A History of Missouri: Volume II, 1820 to 1860*. Columbia: University of Missouri Press, 1971.

McLean, Doug. "Maple Bluff." *Historic Madison: A Journal of the Four Lakes Region* 12 (1995): 3–17.

McClure, Harlan E. *A Guide to the Architecture of the Twin Cities*. New York: Reinhold Publishing, 1955.

McKee, James L. *Lincoln, the Prairie Capital: An Illustrated History*. Northridge, Calif.: Windsor Publications, 1984.

McLaughlin, Robert. *The Heartland: Illinois, Indiana, Michigan, Ohio, Wisconsin*. Time-Life Library of America. New York: Time, 1967.

Meyer, Duane. *The Heritage of Missouri*. Saint Louis: State Publishing, 1963.

Milton, John R. *South Dakota: A Bicentennial History*. New York: Norton, 1977.

Mollenhoff, David V. *Madison: A History of the Formative Years*. Dubuque, Iowa: Kendall/Hunt Publishing, 1982.

Morrison, Maxine. *Nebraska Centennial First Ladies' Cookbook*. Lincoln: Nebraska Centennial, 1966.

Muilenburg, Grace, and Ada Swineford. *Land of the Post Rock: Its Origins, History, and People*. Lawrence: University Press of Kansas, 1975.

Nesbit, Robert C. *Wisconsin: A History*. Madison: University of Wisconsin Press, 1989.

Nichols, Alice. *Bleeding Kansas*. New York: Oxford University Press, 1954.

"North Dakota's First Executive Residence: A Preliminary Historical Survey." [State Historical Society and Society for the Preservation of the Former Governor's Mansion, ca. 1975].

Ohman, Marian M. *Twenty Towns: Their Histories, Town Plans, and Architecture*. Columbia: University of Missouri–Columbia, Extension Division, 1985.

Olson, Charlotte M. "Tour the Governor's Residence." *Perhamm Enterprise Bulletin*, April 17, 1980.

Olson, James C. *History of Nebraska*. 2d ed. Lincoln: University of Nebraska Press, 1966.

Overman, William D. *Ohio Town Names*. Akron, Ohio: Atlantic Press, 1959.

Park, Eleanora G., and Kate S. Morrow. *Women of the Mansion, Missouri, 1821–1936*. Jefferson City: Midland Printing, 1936.

Parker, Nathan H. *The Minnesota Handbook for 1856–7*. Mid-American Frontier. 1857. Reprint, New York: Arno Press, 1975.

Parrish, William E. *A History of Missouri: Volume III, 1860 to 1875*. Columbia: University of Missouri Press, 1973.

Past and Repast: The History and Hospitality of the Missouri Governor's Mansion. Jefferson City: Missouri Mansion Preservation, 1983.

Pease, Theodore Calvin. *The Story of Illinois*. Chicago: University of Chicago Press, 1965.

Peckham, Howard H. *Indiana: A Bicentennial History*. New York: Norton, 1978.

Peirce, Neal R., and Jerry Hagstrom. *The Book of America: Inside 50 States Today*. New York: Norton, 1983.

Perrin, Richard W. E. *The Architecture of Wisconsin*. Madison: State Historical Society of Wisconsin, 1967.

Petersen, William J. *The Story of Iowa*. Volume 1. New York: Lewis Historical Publishing, 1952.

Phillips, Clifton J. *Indiana in Transition: The Emergence of an Industrial Commonwealth, 1880–1920*. Indianapolis: Indiana Historical Society, 1968.

Phillips, Steven J. *Old-House Dictionary: An Illustrated Guide to American Domestic Architecture*. Lakewood, Colo.: American Source Books, 1989.

Poeschl, Peg. "Housing Nebraska's Governors, 1854–1980." *Nebraska History* 61, no. 3 (fall 1980): 259–79.

Porter, Phil. *View from the Veranda: The History and Architecture of the Summer Cottages on Mackinac Island*. Reports in Mackinac History and Archaeology, no. 8. Lansing, Mich.: Mackinac Island State Park Commission, 1981.

Pratt, LeRoy G. *Discovering Historic Iowa: Bicentennial Edition*. Des Moines: State of Iowa, 1975.

Rezatto, Helen Graham. *The Making of the Two Dakotas*. Lincoln: Media Publishing, 1989.

Richmond, Nel Lindner, ed. *Kansas First Families at Home: Residences, Residents, and Recipes*. 2d ed. Topeka: Friends of Cedar Crest Association, 1993.

Richmond, Robert W. *Kansas: A Land of Contrasts*. Saint Charles, Mo.: Forum Press, 1974.

Rifkind, Carole. *A Field Guide to American Architecture*. New York: New American Library, 1980.

Riley, Marianna. "Missouri's Mansion." *Missouri Life* 3, no. 6 (January–February 1976): 26–35.

Robinson, Elwyn B. *History of North Dakota*. Lincoln: University of Nebraska Press, 1966.

Roseboom, Eugene H., and Francis P. Weisenburger. *A History of Ohio*. Rev. ed. Columbus: Ohio Historical Society, 1969.

Roth, Leland M. *A Concise History of American Architecture*. New York: Harper and Row, 1979.

——— . *McKim, Mead, and White, Architects*. New York: Harper and Row, 1983.

Rybczynski, Witold. *City Life: Urban Expectations in a New World*. New York: Scribner, 1995.

Sachs, David H., and George Erlich. *Guide to Kansas Architecture.* Lawrence: University Press of Kansas, 1996.

Sage, Leland L. *A History of Iowa.* Ames: Iowa State University Press, 1974.

Samuelson, Robert E. *Architecture: Columbus.* Columbus: Foundation of the Columbus Chapter of the American Institute of Architects, 1976.

Sandeen, Ernest R. *St. Paul's Historic Summit Avenue.* St. Paul, Minn.: Macalester College, 1978.

Schell, Herbert S. *History of South Dakota.* 3d ed. Lincoln: University of Nebraska Press, 1975.

Schuler, Harold H. *Pierre since 1910.* Freeman, S.D.: Pine Hill Press, 1998.

Schwieder, Elmer, and Dorothy Schwieder. *A Peculiar People: Iowa's Old Order Amish.* Ames: Iowa State University Press, 1975.

Scully, Vincent J., Jr. *The Shingle Style and the Stick Style: Architectural Theory and Design from Richardson to the Origins of Wright.* Rev. ed. New Haven: Yale University Press, 1971.

Sears, Alfred Byron. *Thomas Worthington: Father of Ohio Statehood.* Columbus: Ohio State University Press, 1958.

Seely, Ron. *Madison and Dane County.* Helena, Mont.: American and World Geographic Publishing in cooperation with Wisconsin State Journal and the Capital Times, 1993.

Shortridge, James R. *The Middle West: Its Meaning in American Culture.* Lawrence: University Press of Kansas, 1989.

Small, Nora Pat. "Cedar Crest." *Kanhistique* [Kansas State Historical Society] April 1982, 7–9.

Smith, Alice E. *The History of Wisconsin.* Vol. 1, *From Exploration to Statehood.* Madison: State Historical Society of Wisconsin, 1973.

———. *James Duane Doty: Frontier Promoter.* Madison: State Historical Society of Wisconsin, 1954.

Smith, G. E. Kidder. *A Pictorial History of Architecture in America.* Vol. 2. New York: American Heritage Publishing, 1976.

———. *Source Book of American Architecture: 500 Notable Buildings from the 10th Century to the Present.* New York: Princeton Architectural Press, 1996.

Snyder, John Francis. *Adam W. Snyder and His Period in Illinois History, 1817–1842.* Virginia, Ill.: E. Needham, Bookseller and Stationer, 1906.

Socolofsky, Homer E. *Kansas Governors.* Lawrence: University Press of Kansas, 1990.

Steiner, Jean, ed. *Minnesota Times and Tastes: Recipes and Menus Seasoned with History from the Minnesota Governor's Residence.* St. Paul, Minn.: 1006 Summit Avenue Society, 1993.

Stevens, John H. *Personal Recollections of Minnesota and Its People, and Early History of Minneapolis.* Minneapolis: Marshall Robinson, 1890.

STL [St. Louis Educational and Public Television Commission] 3, no. 1 (January 1993).

"Terrace Hill: A Victorian Jewel." *Transmission* [Northern Natural Gas Co., Omaha] 20, no. 4 (1971): 2–5.

Thomson, Linda K. "Terrace Hill: A Magnificent Gift to the State of Iowa." *Annals of Iowa* 41, no. 4 (spring 1972): 889–917.

Thwaites, Reuben Gold. *Wisconsin: The Americanization of a French Settlement.* Boston:

Houghton Mifflin, 1908.

Transactions of the Illinois State Historical Society. Publication no. 9, Springfield, 1904.

Trutter, John Thomas, and Edith English Trutter. *The Governor Takes a Bride: The Celebrated Marriage of Cora English and John R. Tanner, Governor of Illinois, 1897–1901.* Carbondale: Southern Illinois University Press, 1977.

Tuttle, Charles Richard. *General History of the State of Michigan.* Detroit: R. D. S. Tyler, 1874.

Updegrave, Walter L. "How Our Governors Live It Up." *Money,* October 1993, 115–28.

Upton, Dell. *Architecture in the United States.* Oxford: Oxford University Press, 1998.

Vexler, Robert I. *Chronology and Documentary Handbook of the State of Nebraska.* New York: Oceana Publications, 1978.

Wall, Joseph Frazier. *Iowa: A Bicentennial History.* New York: Norton, 1978.

Weeks, George. *Stewards of the State: The Governors of Michigan.* Ann Arbor: Detroit News and Historical Society of Michigan, 1991.

Whiffen, Marcus, and Frederick Koeper. *American Architecture, 1607–1976.* Cambridge: MIT Press, 1981.

Whittemore, Margaret. *Sketchbook of Kansas Landmarks.* Topeka: College Press, 1936.

Wilkins, Robert P., and Wynona H. Wilkins. *North Dakota: A Bicentennial History.* New York: Norton, 1977.

Williams, Nancy Greenwood. *First Ladies of Wisconsin: The Governors' Wives.* Kalamazoo, Mich.: Ana Publishing, 1991.

Williams, Walter. *The State of Missouri.* Columbia, Mo.: Press of E. W. Stephens, 1904.

Williams, Walter, and Floyd Calvin Shoemaker. *Missouri, Mother of the West.* Vols. 1 and 2. Chicago: American Historical Society, 1930.

Wilson, William E. *Indiana: A History.* Bloomington: Indiana University Press, 1966.

Winckler, Suzanne. *The Great Lakes States.* Smithsonian Guide to Historic America. New York: Stewart, Tabori and Chang, 1989.

———. *The Plains States.* Smithsonian Guide to Historic America. New York: Stewart, Tabori and Chang, 1990.

Withey, Henry F., and Elsie Rathburn. *Biographical Dictionary of American Architects (Deceased).* Los Angeles: Hennessey and Ingalls, 1970.

Wofford, Theodore J., of Murphy, Downey, Wofford, and Richman Architects. "The Missouri Executive Mansion: A Long Range Development Study," Jefferson City: Missouri Mansion Preservation, 1976.

Wyman, Mark. *Immigrants in the Valley: Irish, Germans, and Americans in the Upper Mississippi Country, 1830–1860.* Chicago: Nelson-Hall, 1984.

Zielinski, John M. *Portrait of Iowa.* Minneapolis: Adams Press, 1974.

Zornow, William Frank. *Kansas: A History of the Jayhawk State.* Norman: University of Oklahoma Press, 1957.

Index

Johnson, Carl A., 140
Jones, Thomas D., 9

Kahn, Albert, 57
Kansas: capital of, 44; statehood for, 2, 44. *See also* specific governors
Kansas governor's mansion: architect and architectural style of current mansion, 43, 46; construction date of current mansion, 2, 43, 46; cost of current mansion, 43; current mansion (Cedar Crest; 1962 to present), 44, 45–48, *49–53;* debate on preservation of, 45–46, 47; dining room of, 47, *49;* donation of current mansion (Cedar Crest), 2, 45–47; exterior views of, *50–51, 53;* fence surrounding, 47–48; first mansion (Bennett House; 1901–1962), 44–45, 46; furniture style of current mansion, 43, 48, *49, 52;* interior decor of, 47, 48, *49, 52;* living room of, *52;* location of current mansion, 43, 48; park surrounding, 47, 48; renovation of, 46, 47–48; size of current mansion, 43; thistle motif in, 46, 47
Kappa Kappa Gamma Fraternity, 120
Kaskaskia, Ill., 5
Kelly, Harry F., 58
Kennedy, Jacqueline, 1–2, 8–9, 142
Kennett Castle, 78
Kerner, Otto, Jr., 8
Kidder Smith, G. E., 35
Knowles, Dorothy, 141–42, 143
Knowles, Warren P., 141
Kohler, Walter J., 140
Kohler, Mrs. Walter J., 140

LaFollette, Phillip, 140
Lake Mendota, 139, 140–41, *144–45*
Lake Monona, 139
Landon, Alf, 45
Lansing, Mich., 55, 57
Lausche, Frank, 120
L'Enfant, Pierre, 18, 139
Leonhard and Askew, 109
LeVander, Harold, 68
LeVander, Mrs. Harold, 68
Lewis and Clark expedition, 77, 96, 110, 131, 132
Lincoln, Abraham, 5, 9–10, *15,* 130
Lincoln, Mary Todd, 9
Lincoln, Nebr., 96, 100
Lindenberg, Charles H., 120

Lindenberg House, 120
Link, Arthur A., 109
Little Big Horn, Battle of, 130
Louisiana Purchase, 31, 65, 77
Louisiana Territory, 77

Mackinac Island, 55, 56, 58–59, *63*
Mackinac Island State Park Commission, 58–59
MacLennan, Frank, 45, 46
MacLennan, Marge, 45, 46–47
MacLennan House, 45–47
MacLennan Park, 47, 48
Madison, James, 5
Madison, Wis., 139, 140, 143
Martin birdhouse, *136*
Marx, Karl, 31
Matteson, Joel A., 5
Menninger Clinic, 46
Meridian Street (Indianapolis), 19–21
Meridian Street Foundation, 21
Meridian Street Historic Preservation Commission, 21
Michigan: capital of, 55; size of, 55; statehood for, 2, 55; territory of, 55; Upper and Lower Peninsulas of, 55. *See also* specific governors
Michigan governor's mansion: architects and architectural style of year-round and summer mansions, 54, 57, 59; bar in Lansing residence, 57–58; chandelier in, 58; construction dates of year-round and summer mansions, 54; costs of year-round and summer mansions, 54, 58–59; date completed, 2; dining room of Lansing residence, *61;* donation of, 2, 56–57; exterior view of Lansing residence, *60;* exterior view of summer residence, *63;* foyer of Lansing residence, 57; furniture styles of year-round and summer mansions, 54, 58, 59; gadgets and motorized conveniences in Lansing residence, 57–58; gardens and grounds of Lansing residence, 57; Lansing year-round residence, 2, 54, 56–58, *60–62;* living room of Lansing residence, 57, *61;* locations of year-round and summer mansions, 54, 57, 59; size of year-round and summer mansions, 54, 58, 59; summer residence (Mackinac Island), 2, 54, 55, 56, 58–59, *63*
Michigan Territory, 55
Milliken, William, 58
Minnesota: capital of, 65; settlement of, 65; state-